GERONTOLOGICAL PSYCHOLOGY

Gerontological

Psychology

By

JAMES H. BARRETT, Ed.D

*Director, Southern Colorado
Gerontological Institute
Chairman, Division of Behavioral Sciences
Professor of Psychology
Southern Colorado State College
Pueblo, Colorado*

With a Foreword by

Theodore C. Kahn, Ph.D., D.Sc.

*Head, Department of Behavioral Sciences
Southern Colorado State College
Pueblo, Colorado*

CHARLES C THOMAS • PUBLISHER
Springfield • *Illinois* • *U.S.A.*

Published and Distributed Throughout the World by

CHARLES C THOMAS • PUBLISHER
BANNERSTONE HOUSE
301-327 East Lawrence Avenue, Springfield, Illinois, U.S.A.

NATCHEZ PLANTATION HOUSE
735 North Atlantic Boulevard, Fort Lauderdale, Florida, U.S.A.

This book is protected by copyright. No part of it may be reproduced in any manner without written permission from the publisher.

© 1972, *by* CHARLES C THOMAS • PUBLISHER

Standard Book Number: 398-02226-7

Library of Congress Catalog Card Number: 70-175067

With **THOMAS BOOKS** *careful attention is given to all details of manufacturing and design. It is the Publisher's desire to present books that are satisfactory as to their physical qualities and artistic possibilities and appropriate for their particular use.* **THOMAS BOOKS** *will be true to those laws of quality that assure a good name and good will.*

Printed in the United States of America
PP-22

This book is dedicated to Anna, Cora, George, Harriet, Mart, Chick, Bess and Nell, the octagenarian and nonogenarian family members who were the first models for this study of the developmental and psychological functioning of the aged; and to Louise, Beverly and Coralee, the author's wife and daughters who provided encouragement so necessary to any major effort.

FOREWORD

IN the six or so years that I have known Dr. James H. Barrett I have learned that he is one of those unusual persons who constantly searches out new ideas. He combines innovation with an ability to go to the heart of a matter without getting sidetracked by nonessential details. His book reflects both of these excellent qualities.

After a thorough search of the available literature, which he found wanting, Dr. Barrett includes in his book information on that aspect of aging which the average writer on the subject has consistently omitted. I refer to the normal aspect of aging, to aging and delinquency, and to other topics that are important but which cannot easily be found in the contemporary writings. Dr. Barrett's book is a well-balanced treatment without the usual distorted emphasis on the morbid and sensational aspects of aging.

The book shows evidence of Dr. Barrett's many years of successful teaching experiences and his training as a psychologist. He communicates lucidly and his insights into his subject are penetrating. The book is a work of high scholarship. It synthesizes the current knowledge and research on the subject of gerontology and blends these with the author's own original ideas. That is why its contents will have sustaining appeal for those members of our society about whom the book has been written as well as for the wide spectrum of readers who would like to gain a deeper understanding of this increasingly important segment of our population.

THEODORE C. KAHN

PREFACE

THIS volume is a product of a deep-rooted belief that there is a true need for a book describing the normal geronto, his development and psychological functioning. The author has had an opportunity to study some twenty family members ranging in age from seventy-five to ninety-five. Two of this group became senescent after age eighty-five; all others retained their mental faculties until the very end of life. A mother-in-law at ninety-five and a mother at ninety *still have better memories* than does the author. All of these longevous persons have been able to care for themselves until extreme old age.

Comparisons of this group with the stereotypic elderly individuals generally considered in the literature shows few points of similarity. In order to determine if his relatives were other than normal, the author conducted an evaluation of 159 persons ranging in age from sixty-five to one hundred and one, and found *only* 10 per cent to be like the usual stereotype.

This book, then, is an attempt to provide a true picture of normal aged persons. These are the people who live in their own homes (possibly in retirement villages), remain self-sufficient except in some minor areas like transportation, and are not indigent. Many of this group have their problems too, but they are different problems. The author sincerely hopes that this book may provide another picture of the older American.

JAMES H. BARRETT

INTRODUCTION

MUCH research has been conducted and rather good understandings developed in many of the disciplines concerned with the problems of the older citizen. Geriatric medicine, social work, psychiatry and biology have been studied for a number of years, and authorities have gathered a significant body of knowledge relative to the "care and feeding of the old." There is, however, an almost complete dearth of information concerning the older person as a *human being*.

The writer should like to suggest that *old age is merely one of the important developmental periods in the life span*. While a truly unique period, it is the culmination of the experiences of total life and not something apart from the past. In many respects this a regressive period that may be so, at least partially, because of social imposition. Regressive or progressive, it is a misunderstood and somewhat frightening segment of man's life.

While many object to the so-called fragmentation of the developmental cycle, there are definite segments which are rather complete in themselves. These should be studied as the unique periods they are, but not in isolation. Their relationships to each of the other periods must always be considered and a logical progression maintained.

From maturity until death there are several segments of that total period known as old age. Terminology is presently confused. The definition of geriatric is simple, "the science or art of aging," but the accepted meaning implies physical disability and illness. Senescent, by definition, means "growing old, aging," but the usual connotation is of mental instability and emotional decline. Since this is true, gerontology is one remaining term without restrictive connotation and should probably be used to describe the total developmental period following adulthood.

Despite the certainty that the suggestion will annoy those

who become frenzied about fragmentation, the writer should like to suggest that three truly logical sections of the gerontological period probably exist. These are developmental sections based on individual performance and maturity. Much variation will be found in the individual's rate of development, but progress through these sections will normally take place at certain ages. These divisions can only be made if we remember that the age factor is not sacrosanct and that the *stage*—not the *age*—is the important consideration. The following major sections within the gerontological period seem pertinent:

      58–68 The period of *Later Maturity*
      68–78 The *Early Longevous* period
      78–? The *Later Longevous* period

The term *longevous*, which is, of course, derived from the word longevity, is used by Russian gerontologists and has been adopted by this writer because it has no confusing connotations.

That time, then, from approximately age fifty-eight until death is the gerontological period. The terms suggested for specific areas denote normal behavior and performance through the life span. An individual may develop *senilism* or *senium praecox* (the medical terms used to denote early senility) and become completely senile by age thirty-five or, because of debilitating illness, become geriatric at an equally early age. On the other hand, he may never become a geriatric case or senescent even though he lives to be a centenarian.

Probably the only people in the entire world who understand the problems of the old are the old. It would be easy to sit in a comfortable chair and write a treatise on gerontological psychology. It would, however, be like many books already on the shelves—another volume about a misunderstood subject by a misinformed author—and would certainly lead to further confusion.

In order to provide pertinent knowledge concerning the psychological problems of the elderly and to develop some basic understandings concerning motivating forces, needs, drives, and levels of functioning, the writer has tried to tap the only truly authentic source of fact—*the old themselves*. Information has been gathered concerning such basics as the strengths and weaknesses of the elderly, the developmental tasks of the gerontological period, and changes to be expected in psychological functioning.

Above all, the writer hopes to completely disprove the misleading concepts of the aged accepted by a majority of the population. As an example, one of the major stereotypes of the elderly person is based on the supposition that he is poor, ill, friendless, unable to make his own decisions and merely waiting for death to relieve the tedium of his existence. While this is considered to be the true picture by a majority of our informed (?) citizenry, it is *fact* in no more than 10 per cent of the total population sixty-five and older.

In Appendix A will be found a proposed new stereotype of the older American drawn from information gathered by the writer in a recent study. This provides a rather accurate portrait of the older American as he exists in almost 90 per cent of the gerontological population. An abstract of the complete study from which the new stereotype has been drawn is presented in Appendix B.

In this age of youth, we have almost ignored the existence of the old. We must now evolve more realistic understandings of the true needs of this growing segment of the populace. In addition, we must indoctrinate the total population to a realization of the great potential presently being lost to society by relegating those over age sixty-five to the discard.

ACKNOWLEDGMENTS

ALTHOUGH one person, the author, bears the responsibility for writing a book, it never appears in print without the help of countless other people; colleagues, friends, students and especially those who are required to live with the author during the period of gestation. My special thanks must go to my colleagues, Drs. Maurice L. Howard, Donald D. Megenity, Theodore C. Kahn, Harold Hobbs, Harold Hoeglund, and William S. Keezer, who read, criticized, suggested and evaluated each of the many manuscript revisions and to my wife and daughters who assisted in the editing. To Sharon Pruett, Jean Martinet, and Joan Carlson, who typed the manuscript and to the students who have been exposed to these concepts in classes in gerontological psychology, the author extends his gratitude.

J. H. B.

CONTENTS

	Page
Foreword—THEODORE C. KAHN	vii
Preface	ix
Introduction	xi
Acknowledgments	xv

PART I
DEVELOPMENT IN THE GERONTOLOGICAL YEARS

Chapters
One.	THE PROBLEM	5
Two.	THE DEVELOPMENTAL TASKS OF THE GERONTO	9
Three.	THE OLDER AMERICAN—AREAS OF STRENGTH	28
Four.	THE OLDER AMERICAN—AREAS OF WEAKNESS	37
Five.	SOCIOPSYCHOLOGICAL CHANGE	47

PART II
CHANGES IN PSYCHOLOGICAL FUNCTION

Six.	CHANGES IN SENSORY EXPERIENCE AND PERCEPTION	59
Seven.	CHANGES IN MOTIVATION	70
Eight.	AWARENESS IN THE GERONTOLOGICAL PERIOD	77
Nine.	SHORT-TERM AND LONG-TERM MEMORY	81
Ten.	ADJUSTMENT IN LATER LIFE	87
Eleven.	THE PERSONALITY OF THE GERONTO	98
Twelve.	BIOLOGICAL AGING	113
Thirteen.	AGING AND DELINQUENCY	120
Fourteen.	THE RETIREMENT SYNDROME	132

Selected Bibliography	141
Appendix A—A Portrait of the Older American	145
Appendix B—The Nonpathological Geronto	149
Glossary	160
Index	163

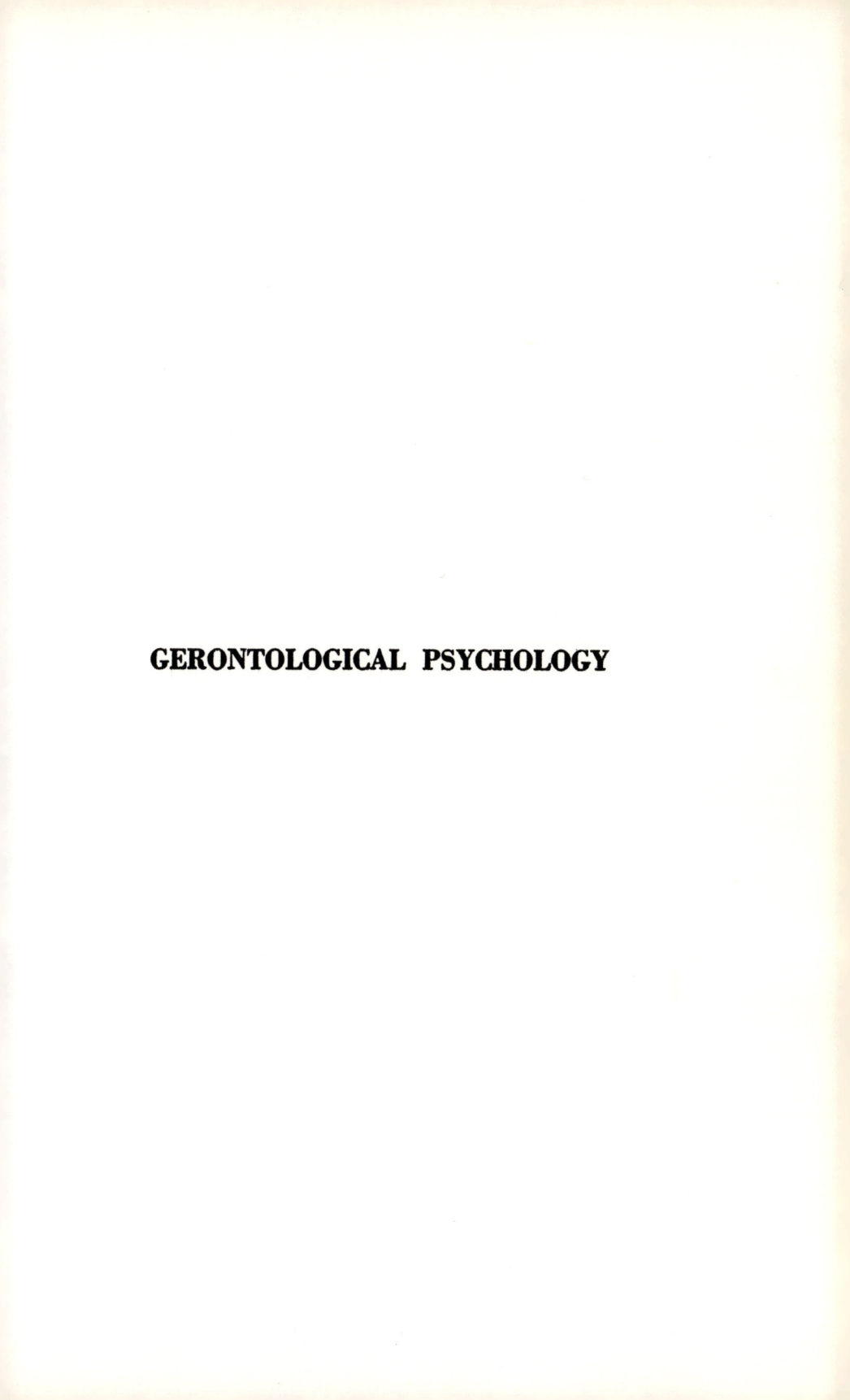

GERONTOLOGICAL PSYCHOLOGY

Part I
Development in the Gerontological Years

Chapter One

THE PROBLEM

ONE of the largest subcultures in the United States today is the subculture of the aged. Some 20 million individuals belong to this socially imposed confraternity. They do not choose to be separated from the mainstream of life, but through mandatory retirement and the national trend toward a *society of youth* have, in far too many cases, been relegated to the discard.

Attempts are continually made to integrate certain of the subcultures into total society. Ethnic and political elements are wooed on every hand and subsidies provided to attract them. Despite repeated overtures, members of many subcultures tend to remain "anti-establishment" and genuine disruptive forces bent on the overthrow of the status quo. It seems something of a paradox that society subsidizes its detractors and offenders while turning its back on over 20 million friends who wish to continue their contributions to the larger community.

Traditionally, the old retained their place in the family circle and frequently assumed patriarchal and matriarchal roles. They were deferred to in major decision-making and their advice sought in matters of importance. Until they died, became chronically ill and/or senescent (in the connotative sense of the word) or retired from *personal choice,* they remained active in their business, profession or trade. Their knowledge, experience and insights more than compensated for any loss sustained because of age.

The tendency to superannuate those over sixty-five is a new social development. It stems from the practice of industry to retire older workers who are replaced with potentially more productive young people. Pension systems and social security have been developed to provide a paltry subsistence level of financial protection. From industry the practice of retiring older individuals spread to business, public employment and the professions. Today only those who are self-employed can expect to escape at least some level of retirement at age sixty-five. Consideration is being given in some areas toward even earlier imposed leisure.

While optional abdication at any age is wonderful, many feel that mandatory retirement tends to be discrimination in its truest sense. It has been suggested that not more than 10 per cent of the population sixty-five and over are in an adequate position financially to live at their pre-retirement standard. Since this is true, the post-retired person living at a substandard level is infrequently happy or content. He believes that he deserves better treatment from the society to which he has contributed so generously throughout his life.

Social change has made it almost impossible to keep the older members in the family home. Houses today are designed with a limited number of bedrooms for small family living. Retirement villages and senior citizens apartments have been constructed throughout the United States as *ghettos for the old*. Many of these provide barely adequate but low-cost housing for older Americans outside the mainstream of life. Only the affluent 10 per cent are able to continue performing at their pre-retirement level. Thus, separated from society, many live out their unhappy, dissatisfied, comfortless years. Though they long for contacts with younger, stimulating individuals, their associates are largely other gerontos with the same problems, the same types of illness and the same outlook on life.

When the old become ill, they must be sent to hospitals, long-term care facilities or nursing homes. Even should the younger family members wish to care for them, it is not usually possible. Since we live in a two-income economy, no one would be at home (even if there was room) to care for the old person. Life in the normally sterile environment found in any institution may be physically adequate but certainly not stimulating or even remotely homelike.

Thus, it would seem that well or ill, the average geronto is exiled to an unsatisfactory environment during the period so often referred to by the euphemistic term, the "golden years."

The gerontological group is large enough today to be an important political force. Should these people become as activist-minded as many members of the other subcultures, their influence would be felt at every level of government and could well prove the deciding voice in numerous areas of decision-making.

It may be pertinent to suggest that society reevaluate the potential of the geronto and make a careful appraisal of his present position in the social structure. In all probability, these steps would result in a new understanding of the older American and possibly lead to an attempt to reintegrate him into the total community.

The prime obstacle to correcting the plight of the aged lies in the almost total lack of knowledge concerning the psychological, social, economic and personal changes that transpire after retirement. While many understandings do exist in the areas of geriatrics, senescence and indigence, only a scant 10 per cent of the total population sixty-five and older belong to the group that are ill, mentally incompetent and financially dependent on society. This small branch is, however, receiving far better treatment from society than the larger nonpathological section that makes up the 90 per cent segment.

The numerous strengths of the geronto must be ascertained together with his inherent weaknesses. If they can be developed, methods of maximizing the strengths and minimizing the weaknesses will assist the older citizen in the achievement of a higher level of personal adjustment. In addition, areas may be suggested in which the aged may well become involved with society.

As one moves through the gerontological period, many new developmental tasks must be mastered if psychological and social adjustment are to be achieved. Certain of these tasks, e.g. accepting and adjusting to the debilitating body and readjustment in the dependence-independence pattern of living, may be considered regressive. The same tasks in their progressive mode were mandatory achievements during the various preadult developmental stages.

Other tasks, not necessarily regressive, are probably best described as compensatory. Among these we find initiating a new search for status, adjusting to changing environments and adjusting to the changing mores of society.

Many times individuals will need help from family and friends in achieving these necessary tasks. The more intelligent, better educated individual who was well-adjusted in adult life will, in most instances, master each new task without help and probably without even recognizing that any adjustment has been effected.

Many basic psychological changes take place during the gerontological periods. Few transpire during later maturity, but become apparent in the early longevous years. Psychologists (both developmental and experimental) have neglected these particular periods in favor of the early developmental years. Countless studies have been made in the fields of childhood and adolescence, and a wealth of experimental data is available in almost every conceivable psychological area as related to these age groups. Certain assumptions do, of course, exist concerning the changes that may be expected in the geronto. Little experimental data are available to substantiate what are merely hypotheses. In many important areas not even postulates exist.

Information is presently available concerning certain of the psychological functions of the old. It is, in most instances, hidden in the general literature and must be sifted out and collated. Through observation, interrogation and experimentation, missing elements must be supplied to complete our understandings of the normal changes in all functions which may be imputable to aging.

Only when society is able to understand the many problems of the older American and when the geronto is inspired to reach a high level of self-understanding, will an unnecessary and somewhat degrading subculture cease to exist. This rather large group will then be returned to its rightful place in total society.

Chapter Two

THE DEVELOPMENTAL TASKS OF THE GERONTO

A DEVELOPMENTAL task is a task which arises at or about a certain period in the life of an individual, successful achievement of which leads to happiness, good adjustment to society and self, and to success with later tasks. On the other hand, failure leads to unhappiness, maladjustment, disapproval by society and difficulty with later developmental problems.

A group of professional workers known as the Committee on Human Development at the University of Chicago* spent many years evolving the concept of "developmental tasks as a means of providing a framework within which they could organize knowledge about human behavior...."

Since this comprehensive study of the tasks, many developmental psychologists have sponsored the concept. Until the present time the developmental tasks have been considered only as they have related to prematurity growth. Many have presently been identified. Among the first were:

1. Achieving an appropriate dependence-independence pattern of living.
2. Achieving an appropriate giving-receiving pattern of affection.
3. Relating to changing social groups.
4. Learning one's psycho-socio-biological sex role.
5. Developing a conscience.
6. Developing an appropriate symbol system and conceptual abilities.

Just how many tasks have been identified up to the present time would be difficult to estimate. Each authority would present

---

*Blair, Arthur Witt, and Burton, William H.: *Growth and Development of the Preadolescent.* New York, Appleton-Century-Crofts, 1961, p. 189.

a different listing with, of course, many items common to all. Some would be indispensable, while others might be of questionable value to many individuals.

The developmental tasks have always been considered solely as steps to maturity. All are of a progressive nature and culminate in adulthood. The level of maturity obtained may well be determined by the number of tasks mastered and the effectiveness of mastery. The value of individual tasks may vary from person to person and while some seem mandatory, others may be elective.

After adulthood is reached it is doubtful if new tasks will be introduced for some time. Continual modification (not change) will, of course, be required in certain areas.

When the adult moves into the gerontological period (usually during the early longevous segment but, on occasion, in the latter part of late maturity), a new hierarchy of developmental tasks must be mastered. These will be divided into two different types, the regressive and the compensatory. They may be just as important to the attaining of adjustment, social approval and individual happiness by the geronto as the tasks of early years have been found necessary to the achievement of well-balanced maturity.

THE REGRESSIVE DEVELOPMENTAL TASKS

Accepting and Adjusting to a Debilitating Body

One of the important developmental tasks of the formative years is learning to adjust to a changing and maturing body. From birth until complete (physical) maturity the body is in a continual state of change. At birth, the head and eyes are almost two-thirds adult size while some parts (e.g. the cerebral cortex of the brain) may not yet exist. Growth proceeds in a completely uneven manner. Several parts may grow while others remain unchanged. Later those parts which have been growing stand still and other portions develop. As a result, body proportions are in a continuous state of change. This means that when a youngster adjusts to fresh growth, proportions change and new adjustments are again needed.

There are two types of growth: quantitative, which is measurable, and qualitative, which is usually not mensurable. Quantitative is bulk growth while qualitative is functional. The two types of growth are not parallel, and bulk growth increases more rapidly than qualitative growth. Since this is true, bodily efficiency is virtually impossible until maturity.

During the years of adulthood, modifications in the body do take place (e.g. changing weight) but no true alterations are noticed. Thus, readjustments are minimal for many years.

During the period of later maturity, the average individual will experience the first indications of physiological debilitation. These are not especially bothersome but merely precursors of things to come. Perceptual abilities begin to show evidence of decline. Visual problems increase, presbycusis accelerates, tactile experiences impress somewhat less, taste sensations are dulled and olfactory impressions tend to weaken. People do not necessarily experience these losses at the same age, nor will the same balance of debilities develop with all. As in every area of development at every age, individual differences are very extensive.

Many individuals will delay these changes until well into the early longevous period. Those who remain highly active, those in superb health, those who avail themselves of the excellent preventative medicine that is available and those who are conscientious in observing their diet and in using adequate vitamin and mineral supplements may escape significant debilitation until almost unbelievable old age.

When impairment can no longer be postponed (on an individual basis, of course), physical as well as physiological enfeeblement will be noticed. Muscles lose their tonus and tend to atrophy, coordination abates and adipose tissue replaces muscle. Kinesthetic responses are no longer effective and all bodily functions are retarded. Loss continues to spread and, finally, the individual becomes geriatric and/or senescent. Only death can negate this inevitable end. It may be delayed until ninety, one hunderd, or one hundred and ten, but not *forever*.

Personal acceptance of inevitable debilitation is a regressive task that may prove extremely difficult for the geronto to master.

A happy, well-adjusted old age may, however, rest on completion of this difficult task.

Adjustment to a Reduction of Sexuality

There is probably more misinformation and lack of information in the field of "sex after sixty" than in any other area of aging. It is commonly believed that after the menopause a woman's desire and need for intercourse no longer exists. As a result, far too many women truly believe that their femininity disappears and that they become neuters after this traumatic experience. It is also commonly believed that man's desire and physical ability to engage in any sexual activity after middle maturity is lost forever.

A syndrome develops in males sometime between ages forty-five and sixty when they report loss of vigor, easy fatigability, decrease in libido or potentia, difficulty in urination with signs of prostatism and hot flushes. This has become known as the *male climacteric* and, surprisingly, frequently develops at the time the wife is going through the menopause. This phenomenon may be produced by sex steroid hormone deficiency. Many doctors report that patients treated with male sex hormones show almost immediate improvement. It is generally conceded by medical and psychiatric practitioners that while true physical inability to engage in sex may become a problem in the later years, the more common issue is psychological. Richard C. Proctor, M.D. in his "Impotence—a Defense Mechanism"* maintains that while certain physical disorders and prostatic disease may produce impotence, the major causes are psychological. Temporary impotence frequently starts a cycle of periodic impotence during which a man becomes unable to consummate the sexual act. This leads to humiliation over the failure which further impedes the effort. This temporary impotence may be due to the stresses of work, new adjustments, disappointments, extreme fatigue or use of certain medication. These failures and disappointments many times lead to continuing psychological impotence which may well then become permanent. In the age of anxiety in which we are

---

*Proctor, Richard C.: Impotence—a defense mechanism. *Journal of the American Geriatrics Society*, Vol. 17, No. 9, p. 874, Sept., 1969.

now living, the prevalence of impotence is greatly increased. Psychotherapy may be required to correct the problem if it becomes deep-seated.

Misconceptions concerning the menopause produce a majority of the sexual problems of the female. Since the folk concept that the menopause heralds the end of desire is still accepted by many, continued sexual activity may, unfortunately, be considered abnormal. Another folk concept that tends to persist is the belief that only men have true sexual desire and that any woman who admits a need is probably immoral. These two factors inhibit the sexual life of the female.

In pre-Christian days the average life span of a woman was twenty-five years, and at the time of the discovery of America, thirty. Thus, the average woman had not reached the menopause prior to death. Today one may plan on possibly living until age eighty. Since this is true, while women at one time never experienced nonfertile life, today they may live over half of their years following the menopause.

It would seem that with men and women alike the problems of sex in the later years tend to be primarily psychological and only secondarily physiological. It is interesting to study "The Natural History of Sexual Behavior in a Biologically Advantaged Group of Aged Individuals."* In this study it was determined that sexual interest and activity in the aged group existed at the same level reported in their younger years.

	Women	*Men*
Reported no interest in youth	0%	0%
Reported weak interest in youth	26%	5%
Reported moderate interest in youth	42%	15%
Reported strong interest in youth	32%	80%

If a group of men and women in the twenty to thirty-five bracket were to be questioned concerning their interest in sex today, the writer would suggest that the modern woman would admit substantially the same level of interest reported by men. This modification must, of course, be attributed to changed social

---
*Pfeiffer, Eric, Verwoerdt, Adriaan, and Wong, Hsioh-Shan. The natural history of sexual behavior in a biologically advantaged group of aged individuals. *Journal of Gerontology*, Vol. 24, No. 2, p. 193, April, 1969.

and moral concepts, to the emancipation of women and to new evaluations of sex in human life.

Since the range of individual differences in "sex after sixty" is so great, adjustment to a reduction in sexuality becomes a purely personal matter. The geronto should learn to accept not only his own changes, but also those of the spouse. Marital adjustments must then be effected if possible. When debilitation seems too great for adjustment, a competent medical doctor and/or psychiatrist should be consulted and corrective measures determined.

A comfortable well-adjusted life in the longevous years may well depend more on mastery of this developmental task than on any one other factor.

Readjustment in Dependence-Independence Pattern of Living

When a child is born, it is almost completely dependent on others. The only areas of independence are breathing, circulation of blood, digestion, vocalization, elimination and uncoordinated movement. Even in these activities, assistance may be required on occasion.

Each day improvement in the areas suggested above may be noted and a continuing development of new autonomy will be observed. If the parent and/or parent surrogate is patient in permitting growth in independence, improvement may be quite rapid. In too many instances, however, it is much easier to do things for the infant than to permit the first ineffectual attempts which must proceed success. This impedes normal development.

All through infancy, childhood, preadolescence and adolescence, growth in independence continues. The peak attained at the time of maturity will probably be the level at which the individual will function until later maturity or even into the longevous years. In the sophisticated society of today, *complete* independence is virtually impossible. On the other hand, complete dependence is frequently observed. However, in aboriginal, primitive, and, to a major degree, early rural societies, almost complete independence was possible and complete dependence virtually impossible.

Throughout the more productive years of life, few changes in the pattern will be observed. The goal accepted in our complicated social world of a high level of interdependence is reached and generally maintained with only slight variations until well after retirement.

After retirement and relegation to the subculture, the individual tends to become less and less independent and his level of interdependence moves toward the dependence point of the continuum. This development is sponsored by society where the peculiar concept has been accepted that the gerontological population wants direct services rather than an opportunity to provide service to self and to others. The more an individual is served and the less he is permitted to administer to others, the more rapidly he will lose his desire to be interdependent and will accept a dependent role almost without question.

The pathological aged gratefully accept imposed dependence. On the other hand, the larger percentage of the nonpathological segment resist the loss of their interdependent state. Society must resolve its concept of the needs of the geronto and act in accordance with new findings. The older American should be encouraged to retain his dignity and independence as long as possible.

Eventually, of course, every individual (unless death intervenes) will reach a stage where dependence is inescapable. There is usually a gradual decline until complete reliance on others is requisite. During the period of decline the individual must be brought to an acceptance of his changing status. This, then, becomes a developmental task of prime importance and one quite difficult to accept. The geronto must be prepared during his competent years to accept the fact that this regressive task will require mastery in the not too distant future. If he is prepared to expect this problem he will be less resistant and will, in all probability, master the task.

Accepting a Different Role in the Family Circle

This usually proves to be a most difficult task to achieve! When one has been a decision-maker, a provider, a counselor, a nurse, a confidant, a teacher, a disciplinarian, a banker, an employer, and a minor diety, it is difficult to accept a lesser role.

All through the years when the family is "growing up," father and mother play the leading role in a continuing drama of life. Gradually as the children mature, the role changes. When the child becomes a preadolescent, the parents lose their halos. The nursing function tends to be the next to go. One by one the remaining offices disappear until, with complete maturity of the offspring, only the roles of counselor, confidant and possibly banker remain. In many instances even these disappear.

For a long period of time, the adult progenitor remains only a close friend and, on rare occasions, confidant and banker. A reciprocal relationship develops where mutual support becomes the new order. This association is usually satisfying to both parent and progeny.

When the parent reaches the gerontological period of his life, a reversal of roles tends to evolve. As disengagement and occupational and social withdrawal take place, retirement problems become significant. The geronto may lose his confidence and his decision-making ability in many cases and, even when he remains completely competent, he is almost universally conceded to be at least partially incapacitated. As a result, the children begin to usurp parental prerogatives. Eventually an almost complete reversal of roles is effected. This, then, becomes a regressive developmental task that is imposed upon the geronto. As such, mastery is resisted to the bitter end. In many cases children even impose this change through the courts. This is, of course, to be regretted; the writer believes that as long as any level of competence remains the geronto should retain as many functions as possible.

Learning to Accept More Than One Is Capable of Giving

This is a task that may be closely related to the acceptance of a different role. In this case the consideration will not be exclusively a family matter, but will extend to society as a whole.

The geronto who has been giving to individuals, organizations and "causes" throughout his life may find himself in a position where this is no longer possible. Contribution of money is not usually permissible in a retirement budget and gifts of "self" may no longer be requested. This, then, becomes another area where the old become separated from society, and introduces another regressive developmental task. One may even regress to the point where he must accept services from others and, at times, financial aid. In refusing assistance the individual, to retain his self-image, may live in deprivation rather than admit the existence of any need. It is truly regrettable that anyone in modern society must be deprived to maintain his self-respect. This may become a difficult task to accept.

Reorientation to Primary Social Groups

This related task is almost inevitable. When one is an infant, he exists first in an almost one-to-one (mother and child) situation and shortly to a one-to-family situation. This is, of course, a primary social group which provides a comfortable initiation to the world of people. By easy stages (the addition of other relatives, friends of the family, neighbors and Sunday school acquaintances), the infant moves through early childhood to school days.

The individual's sphere continues to grow to include secondary and tertiary groups until the social world is a complex, highly sophisticated world.

Purely social contact, political affiliations, service clubs, fraternal organizations, church membership, educational cliques and business or professional associations provide both breadth and depth to the social world of the individual. Finally, during maturity, the average person accepts his complicated public service function as being the natural way of life and adapts all of his behavior to this role.

When the gerontological years begin, especially following retirement, there is a gradual reduction of affiliations. Usually the first to go are the educational followed shortly by the business or professional. Political and service clubs may continue for a brief period. Social and church associations together with fraternal membership are maintained for many years—probably as long as one remains fairly mobile—but even these disappear in time. This returns the geronto to the life he knew as a child—a very simple primary social, usually face-to-face existence.

This is a bitter pill for many who have valued their complex social acceptance. Frequently older people resist this change more than any other they are forced to make. Mastery of this developmental task is difficult and frequently resisted to the end. The more complex the social group hierarchy during maturity, the more resistant the individual will be when regression becomes necessary.

Other regressive developmental tasks will be found which may be more difficult to achieve than those listed above. Most will be found on an individual basis and may be uniquely related to the life of the individual during the mature years. The reader is encouraged to search for these and to personally evaluate their importance.

COMPENSATORY DEVELOPMENTAL TASKS

The regressive tasks discussed in the preceding section are closely related to the progressive form of the same tasks mastered before maturity. The compensatory tasks, on the other hand, are unique lessons that lead to better adjustment in old age and are not related in any major way to prematurity development. Many of these may be individually rather than collectively important. All should be considered in terms of personal need. Additional areas of compensation will most certainly be observed by the student of gerontology.

Developing New Leisure Time Activities to Meet Changing Abilities

As one enters the gerontological period of life, he will have far more leisure time to pursue hobbies and recreational activities. In all too many cases, the avocations of his active years are no longer appropriate to declining abilities. Other activities, which may be not only appropriate but interesting, are limited by the cost factor when the budget is inadequate. Since gerontological adjustment may well depend on ability to utilize leisure, this becomes a critically important task.

The individual who in youth and early maturity spent much of his leisure time playing tennis may find himself to be physically inadequate when he enters late maturity. His physician warns him that his heart will no longer stand the strain of such strenuous activity. Golf may, in many instances, prove an acceptable substitute for the preferred sport. Later, inability to walk great distances may require the geronto to use a golf cart or to move to shuffleboard.

One who has played the piano or organ may find that an arthritic condition dictates a change of activity. Listening to recordings may replace personal performance, or an instrument requiring less dexterity (e.g. the autoharp) may be substituted. With failing eyesight, talking books and other types of recordings may replace reading as an avocation.

In many cases new activities and hobbies must be suggested to accommodate the changing abilities of the individual. Philately (stamp collecting) is an excellent, relatively inexpensive hobby that almost any older person can enjoy. Various crafts can be made available for those with different talents, abilities and inclinations. In retirement villages and homes and in senior citizens centers, occupational therapy specialists and physical and recreational activities directors should be available to provide guidance in use of leisure time.

Since the retired individual has so much free time to be utilized, this becomes a very critical area. Probably this most important of compensatory developmental tasks may prove one of the more difficult to master.

Learning New Work Skills

The geronto frequently finds that should he wish to become employed on either a full or part-time basis following retirement, opportunities are rarely available in his occupational or professional field. On other occasions the older person may find that he is no longer capable in his vocational calling. In either event he must develop new skills and fresh abilities in areas where opportunities may be available to him.

The individual who has remained in an occupation or profession he detested because of a need for security will welcome an opportunity to try a new vocation. On the other hand, a person who has loved every minute of his career will accept the need for change, but with regret.

The retired geronto who finds employment necessary because of inadequate retirement income or who wants a position to avoid boredom may have a problem. While an employer cannot refuse to hire an individual because of race, creed, color or marital status, he is legally permitted to *discriminate* against one over sixty-five. In this age of youth, all too few new opportunities are available for anyone over forty and in some areas even to those as young as thirty-five. Since this is true, the victims of retirement are usually faced with continuing unemployment.

The only solution may be to search for those employment areas where *demand* exceeds supply. In such fields, if one is mobile and capable, age is no barrier. Where an acceptable opportunity presents itself, the older person may need to be trained or retrained to satisfactorily meet job requirements. Learning new skills may be simple or difficult. If there is a relationship between the new job and former employment, if old skills may be renovated or modified, retraining may be easily accomplished. If, however, the new position is totally unrelated to any former activity and completely new skills must be mastered, training may prove difficult if not impossible.

This particular compensatory task tends to range in difficulty from simple to almost impossible. Its great importance may, however, provide that high level of motivation which is so necessary to the overcoming of obstacles. When even minimal support is provided by society, mastery can usually be assured.

Making Necessary Dietary Adjustments

This may prove to be a major developmental task for many older people. On the other hand, an almost equal number will have little if any difficulty. Adjustment will depend largely on whether the individual in youth and maturity would "eat to live" or "live to eat." Almost all people have certain food preferences and certain distinct dislikes. When the preferences are compatible with the prescribed diet, the geronto is most fortunate. If, however, the required regime consists largely of foods heartily disliked, acceptance is difficult.

Certain ethnic groups have great difficulty in relinquishing the staples of their diets for the bland foods usually suggested by the dietitian as essentials in old age. Of course, the writer's mother, at ninety years of age, still eats hot chili, pizza and fried pork! She apparently thrives on this totally unacceptable diet and would probably die if fed the pap usually recommended for the aged. This might indicate that acceptable diet is a purely individual matter determined by experimentation. Each individual must be led to an acceptance of his limitations and the possible restriction to foods he can tolerate. While a majority of the compensatory tasks present objectional features, to many individuals this is the most distasteful.

Adjusting to Changing Environments

It is interesting to find that the plight of the nonpathological geronto is more frequently considered in the popular press than in more scholarly works. Jeanne Toomey, in a recent article in the *Family Weekly*,* quotes Dr. Theodor Reik, one of Sigmund Freud's earliest and most brilliant pupils and author of *Listening with the Third Ear*. Dr. Reik, now eighty-one, writes, "Do not isolate the older person from society! He should contribute wisdom, stories of other times, advice and counsel to the young who may well profit from his advice." He continues, "This is why I dislike so-called 'Golden Age' housing developments or nursing homes where the main topic is of physical ills."

In the same article, Toomey quotes Dr. Coulter Rule, New York psychologist and consultant to the Presbyterian Home for Aged Women and Peter Cooper Nursing Home. Dr. Rule comments, "When the aged have problems that require them to be fed, for instance, nursing homes are necessary. *But if they are ambulatory* and can arrange to live in a home setting, it's better. The retirement setting should be one in which the older person can watch the kids go back and forth to school from a rocking chair—perhaps not as an active member but as a wise oldster."

---

*Toomey, Jeanne: How you can stay young all your life. *Family Weekly*, August 10, 1969, p. 4.

Both of these authorities are suggesting that today's tendency to ghettoize the old destroys the human ecological balance where people of all ages live in harmony, mutually supportive in all things.

When the geronto is removed from his natural environment to the sterile artificial atmosphere of the *usual* facility provided for the elderly, he is required to accept an almost impossible locale. This becomes a compensatory developmental task that may provide a truly traumatic experience. The pathological geronto adjusts easily and willingly to an environment where direct services become a way of life. The nonpathological older person does not want direct services, but to be provided with means and opportunities to serve self and others. This almost irreconcilable conflict between the philosophy prevalent in the operation of the *average* facility for the aged and those it has been designed to serve, presents almost impossible problems. There are, of course, a limited number of retirement and nursing facilities where the needs of the nonpathological are considered. The criticism noted above is directed at the usual home dedicated to the provision of direct services to the pathological aged.

When adequate facilities are not available and the geronto has no place to go, he must learn to live in an unacceptable environment. The writer can find no solution to the problem and readily concedes that this developmental task may be impossible to achieve.

Adjusting to the Changing Mores of Society

Each generation tends to have problems in understanding and accepting succeeding generations. The major points of contention frequently come from the changing mores (or if you prefer, folkways) accepted by the young. The older people do not, regrettably, remember that their parents had exactly the same difficulty in understanding their youthful practices. The generation gap considered by many to be uniquely of this generation is really as old as time. It is mentioned in the Bible, in hieroglyphics on the walls of King Tut's tomb and in *Poor Richard's Almanac* as written by Benjamin Franklin! Despite the fact that it may date him, the writer would suggest that he can remember when any girl who "bobbed" her hair was sinful, the lady who used any makeup was not a lady and a female who did not wear at least three petticoats (slips) was a "fallen angel"! This is a far cry from today's acceptance of mini skirts, pants suits, elaborate coiffures and professional makeup.

Each new generation starts the adolescent (or perhaps pre-adolescent) years by accepting the standards of the parents. Soon, however, while the adult mores remain fixed as they were at the time the adult reached maturity, the teen peer group members move beyond acceptable limits established by mature standards. They continue to change concepts until they reach maturity when their mores become fixed as were those of their parents. Too often the older generations (parents who do not accept standards of children, and grandparents who may now have two generations with unacceptable practices to condemn) reject the "new society" and refuse to accept the fact that possibly the change may be only *difference* rather than "goodness" or "badness," "morality" or "immorality."

Surprising as it may seem, better rapport frequently exists between the young and their grandparents than between either children and parents or parents and grandparents. This may be true because both the young and the old feel that the middle group are too domineering in their relationships. In addition, the mores may, in certain cases, come full circle in two generations.

While there may be some *modifications* in opinions held by the elders, change is not usually possible. Certain groups, notably teachers, professors and clergymen, (those who have closest contact with younger generations on a broad spectrum) are more open to change and at least partial acceptance of the "new morality."

One of the more difficult developmental tasks of the geronto may well be adjustment to new ideas. This is not, by any stretch of the imagination, personal acceptance of the change (though this may happen on rare occasions) but rather is a realization that others should be allowed to determine their own concepts and not, because of tradition, be required to accept the behavioral practices of their parents and grandparents *who themselves did not accept the mores of their elders.*

Initiating a New Search for Status

The individual who in his years of active employment achieved a satisfactory level of status may in retirement feel little need for rank or position. He may happily relinquish any claims he has had to high acceptance. A residue of status will, of course, remain to that individual who in retirement continues to live in the environment where he achieved his standing.

From early childhood there is usually high-level motivation to achieve a position in the sun. The young attempt, through sports, music, activities and even through educational excellence, to become important in the eyes of their peers. If they fail in all socially acceptable areas, they may move to those that are not acceptable. They often become known as the meanest, the most profane, the most dishonest individuals in their school. Reformatories and penitentiaries are filled with people who made their mark in a variety of unacceptable enterprises.

Many individuals in early maturity accept the fact that achievement of status will probably always escape them. Once reconciled to this plight, all attempts are discontinued. Those who refuse to recognize their inability to achieve by acts may attempt to gain standing through associations. Many believe that affiliation with certain churches, fraternal organizations, service and social clubs will give them an adequate level of reflected status. These persons will probably serve to satisfy need on a permanent basis through these associations.

We find four types of individuals among the retired population: (1) those who have achieved adequate status during maturity and are satisfied in their retirement years with the residue, (2) those who accept inability to achieve any significant "place in the sun," (3) those who achieve adequate satisfaction through affiliation and (4) those who reach the gerontological period still unhappily seeking status. The latter group may become problems to their associates. Opportunities must be provided for these gerontos to become leaders in activities, to become spokesmen for the groups, to contribute to the well-being of those less fortunate than themselves. Such activities may provide *pseudostatus* considered real by the individual. On rare occasions certain of these people will, in a group less able than they themselves, achieve a true level of status.

This, on a purely individual basis, may become a rather important developmental task.

Modifying Individual Self-concepts

As an individual matures, he tends to develop a private world comprised of attitudes, feelings, values, perceptions, desires and expectations. Psychologists have different names for this private world of the individual. Some refer to it as the "self-concept," others as the "self," the "ego," or the "sense of self-identity." These are generally used as interchangeable terms, but somewhat different shades of meaning are probably inherent in the phraseology.

Freud contends that the ego interprets reality to the id (the individual drives and inherited *mass of energy* which strives for expression) so that the latter may be provided with direction. The young and, regrettably, many immature adults have weak egos which fail to exercise important controls over dangerous and/or socially undesirable activities. The superego, in Freudian terminology, is that force which distinguishes between right and wrong. Non-Freudians modify this concept and give is a new label—the conscience.

The writer personally believes that the *self-concept* is more inclusive than the *ego*, the *self*, or the *sense of self-identity* and should not be used with identical connotations. To the elements listed above—attitudes, feelings, values, perceptions, desires, and expectations—should be added conscience, and an understanding of "who one is," "why one is here," "where one lives," and "where one is going." This, then, will form the true self-concept.

The development of an adequate self-concept in an individual is the responsibility of the parent, the teachers, and possibly, the church. This task must be assumed by the person himself as he approaches maturity. Closely related to the self-concept may be the personality. Since the personality of the individual can be described as "the total impact he has on others both individually and in groups," the self-concept is unquestionably reflected in the personality.

The self-concept is an everchanging thing. At about two years of age the youngster discovers self and by three he will say with finality, "I want! I don't want! I like! I don't like! I am not a girl, I am a boy. My name is Joe. This is my ball!" By four he includes others with *we* and *our* in his thinking. Until maturity is reached, a continuing expansion of the self-concept may be expected. Many believe that by age ten, or possibly eleven, a stable, basic self-concept will have been developed.

Wide experience, education in some depth, growing ability to appraise self, complete acceptance of handicaps and impairments (speech problems, poor vision, etc.) together with maximized social interaction, combine to develop in the mature adult a high-level self-concept that leads to excellent social and personal adjustment. Unless some traumatic experiences are suffered during the mature years, the self-concept will remain rather constant. Modifications may take place, but changes are not to be anticipated.

As one enters the longevous years (rarely in later maturity), many alterations take place. Attitudes change, feelings suffer inversion, values shift, perceptions weaken, desires alter and expectations tend to diminish. In addition, the individual may become unsure of just who he is and realize that he is no longer going anywhere. Because of these changed components, the self-concept of the individual regresses to the point that he may consider himself to have no worth. Despite the fact that he may have many talents and remain capable in a variety of areas, losses are magnified to the point that they blind the geronto to his continued worth.

Among the many compensatory developmental tasks, none is more significant than *modifying individual self-concepts*. Nothing remains at seventy or eighty or ninety as it was at twenty or thirty or forty. While one may resist, one cannot always prevent change. As a result, two avenues remain: (1) attempt to delay change by substituting modification, and (2) wherever a change is unavoidable, immediately accept an alternate that is personally acceptable. By following these suggestions, the self-concept will be altered and/or modified, but will remain virtually intact and the individual's personal and social adjustment will not suffer.

In addition to the compensatory tasks listed here that tend to be almost universal, there are many that are important on an individual basis. Others have minimal significance and are not worthy of discussion. Each individual must assess his own needs and when compensation seems necessary, search for available answers. The gerontologist must learn to evaluate the needs of his charges and to develop methods to assist in mastering not only the universal but the personal tasks as well.

If all significant regressive and compensatory developmental tasks are mastered to a satisfactory degree, adjustment in the gerontological years will almost certainly be assured.

Chapter Three

THE OLDER AMERICAN—
AREAS OF STRENGTH

CONTRARY to popular belief based on studies of the stereotypic older person, many strengths may be found in the later years which were not necessarily present in early and middle maturity. New strengths rarely develop in the geriatric and/or senescent population but may be observable in many *non-pathological* gerontos.

As was true in the early years of life, the quantity and quality of development tends to flower in direct ratio to the type of environment provided the individual. A young person who matures in culturally and intellectually deprived environs will rarely achieve to the peak of his abilities. While heredity does determine an individual's latent possibilities, his environment may limit the amount of total potential he will realize. Gerontological development is subject to the same limiting factors. One may have great potential for continuing maturity *after age sixty-five*. As a matter of fact, we find many documented examples of development enduring into the eighties and even the nineties. How long and how fully individual's develop will depend to a great degree on their milieu. It is doubtful if one should expect significant positive change to take place in the average institutional environment.

The following strengths have been identified and observed by the writer in numerous cases. Not all will, as a usual rule, be developed by any one person. Some may achieve only one or two, others a majority of those mentioned. This is not to be considered a complete tabulation. Each reader is encouraged to add other areas he may have observed.

CREATIVITY BASED ON EXPERIENCE

Creativity is a talent which is easy to stifle during the years of childhood and adolescence. If, however, one reaches maturity with the ability to create well-established, it should continue to expand into adulthood and old age. Nearly all children possess keen imagination with creative potential, but factually oriented parents and teachers tend to discourage its logical development.

Uncontrolled imagination may, of course, lead to dependence on fantasy and frequently to bizarre unrealities. This is the phase adults hope to discourage in the young. Too often, however, highly desirable creativity, which is another facet of the same imaginative quality, is also precluded and the "baby is thrown out with the bath water!" Since preventative techniques are so often applied, not more than 20 per cent to 25 per cent of the total adult population retain a significant level of true creativity. Artists, musicians, poets, authors, composers, inventors and innovators almost invariably come from this rather small percentage of the total population.

If an individual becomes senescent in his older years, he will most certainly lose his creativity along with any intellectual potential he may have possessed. On the other hand, if his mind remains functional, as it tends to do with 90 per cent of the group older than sixty-five, creativity may improve in those cases where the individual maintains an adequate level of motivation.

Each challenge an individual experiences provides him with additional frames of reference for understanding and evaluation. Thus, the individual who is truly creative will continue to expand and refine his imagination and inventiveness into the longevous years. Countless examples exist to document this fact. Pablo Picasso, Giuseppe Verdi, Pablo Casals, Thomas Edison and Luther Burbank are excellent examples of creativity continuing to develop and expand into the later longevous period of life. In fact, many of the major accomplishments of these men (and of other creative individuals) were attained after they became octogenarians.

Creativity is an especially fascinating area to consider since it seems to have little correlation with *measurable* intelligence and/or educational achievements. The examples cited above would seem to indicate that this quality is a unique talent which exists independently. The older person fortunate enough to have been endowed with this priceless gift will tend to remain functional and productive to the very end of his life span.

FREEDOM TO CONCENTRATE

The pre-retired person (regardless of age) becomes so involved with his trade, business or profession that he has far too little time to concentrate on anything of an extraneous nature. The intensity of his effort will, through necessity, be directed toward the earning of his livelihood. Growth and personal development tend to be curtailed in too many cases until later maturity. The post-retired individual has sufficient time in which to concentrate if he retains an adequate level of motivation.

Other distracting compulsions may be reduced or eliminated as one becomes older. The psychophysical wants and needs (sex, hunger, rest, activity and so forth) and the psychosocial desires (prestige, power, security, affiliation) may now have reached a level where they continue to motivate but no longer inhibit. The need for status-seeking in cases where retirement follows accomplishment is greatly reduced and will no longer be an obstacle to intensified effort.

Achievements previously unattainable now become possible through the removal of inhibiting and distracting needs. The retirement years for many may become the finest years of self-actualization and fulfillment because of this newly found strength.

FREEDOM FROM SOCIAL PRESSURE

As a general rule, the older individual has been emancipated from a majority of the social pressures that were dominating forces in his youth and early adult years. During those periods the expectations of society determined his observable behavior, even in situations where they were in direct conflict with inner predispositions.

The need to impress others is not usually of paramount importance to the geronto. Pressures to conform are no longer imperatives (unless they are exerted by the spouse!) and personal decisions are usually respected by one's peers. This emancipation from society's almost complete control allows a certain freedom of action impossible to the younger adult.

A minimal level of pressure will still be exerted by the peer group, but since this clique tends to be of the same generation, the coercion is seldom unreasonable. In addition, one may feel free to ignore others of his era if he so chooses.

The competent, talented retiree will continue to be pressured to provide free help to individuals and agencies. Society, while relegating those over sixty-five to retirement, continues to call on them for the valuable services they are still capable of performing. Since they are on pension and/or retirement income, remuneration is rarely suggested.

The older American infrequently feels the need to impress others. This tends to make him immune to a majority of the compulsions applied by society. Pressures the young adult cannot hope to escape can be resisted by one who feels no need to impress.

MATURITY AND WISDOM

Growing old does not, in itself, necessarily insure the development of wisdom. Those with a latent potential to become wise do, however, tend to develop higher levels of sagacity in their longevous years.

In evaluating an individual, one must not mistake high I.Q., educational achievement, cunning, shrewdness, accumulated factual knowledge, erudition or excellence of memory as being synonymous with wisdom. One may have high intellectual capacity, numerous college degrees, be erudite and yet remain foolish rather than wise!

Wisdom per se is difficult to identify and probably more difficult to describe. This writer concluded many years ago that wisdom was nothing more or less than common sense possessed to an uncommon degree. The wisest man may be illiterate but endowed with a basic perceptiveness which makes sagacity possible.

The older person who has discovered many areas of interest during his more active years is truly fortunate. Cross-fertilization among these fields tends to yield gestalt concepts that increase with age. In addition, one who has had wide experience in both related and unrelated areas will have developed countless frames of reference which he may utilize in conceptualization. Thus, while age does not produce wisdom, it will intensify and magnify the quality where it is found to exist.

ADJUSTMENT OF VALUES

As the individual moves into the gerontological period of life, his value system tends to become rather well-defined. In many cases it will be logically organized for the first time after many years of vacillation and indecision.

With maturity, a reconciliation of conflicting beliefs and convictions will frequently be effected and, as a result, the values of the older person tend to become mutually supportive. The discordance so much a part of youth rarely exists into the older ages. When values support each other, personal convictions become strengthened and the individual develops a new depth of character.

The distorted values so commonplace among the intellectually immature have generally disappeared as one moves into later maturity. Seen in proper and logical perspective, new concepts are integrated into the total pattern of understanding.

The psychologically mature individual tends to develop that rather complete system of perception, interpretation and reaction so necessary to the achievement of a normal, effective later life This becomes possible only when an adequate and integrated value system has been evolved.

REVALUATION OF LIFE SPACE

In youth and early maturity, many individuals discover that certain areas of involvement are closed to them. Even if one's motivation is extremely high, a goal outside of his life space is unattainable. One's existence seems to be circumscribed by a variety of factors. Among the restrictive forces will be found level of intelligence, physical and emotional factors, race, color, background of experience, quality of education and individual talents.

The writer in his youth was strongly motivated to become a

concert singer. While he had a fairly adequate voice and a good level of musicianship, he did not possess that extra measure of talent required for the concert stage. This, then, became a career outside of his life space and, therefore, impossible for him to attain. Because of limiting factors which cannot be negated, almost every individual is denied access to areas of personal interest where motivation is high.

During early and middle maturity, most people gradually adjust to an acceptance of self. In many cases, however, the adjustment is merely compromise and life space limitations are not admitted. Rationalization must then be employed to explain facts that are not truly acceptable.

When the individual moves into the gerontological period of life, he gradually learns not only to accept but also to understand the life space that is his. The person who is highly intelligent may begin to understand during the years of early and middle maturity and complete his revaluation of life space during the first years of his retirement.

It is necessary that one sort through his experiences, needs and wants and recognize why opportunities have been limited in numerous areas. With this evaluation will come an acceptance of reality and a new contentment in later life. This phenomenological approach to personal assessment has much to recommend it to the student of gerontology.

PERSONALIZED PROBLEM SOLVING

As a usual rule, the mature individual will have developed his own personalized approach to problem solving. Based on experience and evolved through a process of trial and error, it may prove to be very efficient.

Through trial and error one may develop those comprehensive insights that are indispensable to critical thinking in problem solving. If, however, those insights are not based on logical concepts, but on the verbal habits and associations that are frequently utilized, the conclusions which follow will probably be invalid. Prejudices are frequently used in attempts at problem solving with unacceptable results.

With age the intelligent person will have evaluated the effectiveness of his techniques and will have discarded the ineffectual in favor of the personalized approach resulting from his experience and based on his accumulated knowledge.

A NEW BROAD-MINDEDNESS

The educated individual in his mature years may become more broad-minded. Lines of reasoning now utilize countless frames of reference providing greater breadth of understanding. While conflict may develop in certain learned and/or secondary drives, there is, in general, a noticeable lessening of motivational conflict. In most instances the pressure of the primary homeostatic drives is limited by decreasing physiological need. Certain of the nonhomeostatic drives (e.g. sex) are curbed by social pressure in addition to organic debilitation. Diminishing motivational conflict may lead to broad-mindedness.

The liberal-mindedness of the geronto may not extend to the activities of the adolescent and preadult population due to the inherent conflict of generational mores. When standards of good versus bad, right versus wrong, and moral versus unmoral or immoral are in conflict, mutual understandings are almost impossible. In those professions where contacts and lines of communication remain open between generations, acceptance of changing behavioral patterns may be expected. Teachers, professors, clergymen and medical practitioners are among the more tolerant toward the young and, as a result, usually comprise the most broad-minded segment of the older generation.

A PERSONAL CRITERIA OF REALITY

The older person has usually identified his own criteria of reality. This has come about, at least in part, through personal identification of acceptable authority. The expert accepted by the individual need not be considered as such by others. Reality to one is not necessarily reality to another. To the Christian, God is real and the ultimate authority; to the infidel, Diety does not exist. No two people accept the same hierarchy of authority, nor do they need to do so. Reality to one may be fantasy to another. As long as one is able to identify and accept as valid his own criteria, he will probably become adequately adjusted.

In many cases, the individual's criteria of reality may stem from intuition. This may be an adequate guide for certain introspective people, but should not receive general acceptance. If experience is identified solely through intuition, it may lead to neurotic behavior. This is also true for criteria established as the results of dreams or through the use of narcotics and certain drugs. In a great many cases, revelation may be questioned.

OTHER AREAS OF STRENGTH

There are, of course, many areas of strength not considered above. Some have been pinpointed by the writer, others have not. Among those identified are two that may be quite significant. These tend to be so obvious, however, that they will not be discussed in any great detail here.

1. Solitary pursuits tend to be more acceptable during the gerontological period. This makes possible a higher plateau of introspective planning. In addition, concentrated development of ideas may now be possible at peak levels of performances.

2. The older individual tends to develop patience if he is well-adjusted. The high level of frustration tolerance that may come with age is another factor which contributed to the maturation of this desirable trait. The person who is *not* well-adjusted will, with age, become *very* impatient.

The gerontological period may prove to be a highly productive era in one's life. It may also produce rich rewards in personal growth and individual satisfaction. The above becomes possible only when the individual is highly motivated to remain active and refuses to resign from society as do too many after mandatory retirement.

The older individual must be convinced of his worth and encouraged to continue his participation in a variety of the activities that are still available to him. He must learn to recognize the many powers of the geronto and develop methods of maximizing those that he possesses. The strengths considered in the preceeding material seem to be rather basic. There are, of course, a great many additional areas which may be discovered individually.

Psychologists, sociologists, social workers and others who work with gerontos should search for the strengths possessed in individual areas and help the person to develop roles in terms of observable potential. As strengths are maximized and weaknesses minimized, the older American who is adequately motivated will continue to make a valuable contribution to society.

Chapter Four

THE OLDER AMERICAN— AREAS OF WEAKNESS

STUDIES of the older American reveal many areas of weakness that seem to be inherent. More noticeable, of course, among the geriatric and senescent minority, they tend also to be somewhat prevalent in the nonpathological group. Many of these weaknesses were present in early life, but a majority seem to be a result of the aging process. Few individuals will experience all impairments listed here, but none will escape them all. Some weaknesses are physical, others mental, a few psychological. Regardless of origin, each provides the individual with problems to overcome and areas where compensation becomes necessary.

The environment in which a person lives may prove to be a major factor in the termination or continuation of his development. If one is able to compensate for various weaknesses, one can frequently minimize the adverse effects that might be expected and continue a useful and productive life.

The following areas have been identified and observed by the writer in numerous cases. This is not, of course, a complete listing of potential weaknesses, but does probably contain the most prevalent and critical areas. Each reader should search for other impairments and add to his personal list for consideration.

THE DEBILITATING BODY

Many authorities suggest that the individual's physical peak may be reached at about age nineteen. From this time on there tends to be a gradual decline with many plateaus of varying duration. In later life, the rate of decline becomes accelerated and the plateaus of shorter duration.

In the society of today, the accelerated decline due to physiological change is, in many cases, delayed by good nutrition and preventative medicine. As a result, the independent and productive life span has been greatly increased. However, nothing presently known will prevent declining abilities indefinitely.

As bodily efficiency decreases, handicaps become more apparent. Among the especially significant will be the increase in reaction time with the attendant slowing of reflexes and the retardance of all responses. Many activities must be curtailed due to these changes. As an example, the geronto may become an unsafe driver and possibly lose his facility with tools. Alertness must be greatly increased to compensate for loss.

A second enfeeblement which may be an early indication of approaching debilitation is the loss of the ability to coordinate. When the individual has suffered an acute illness (not the chronic illness of the geriatric), he may, for a period of time, became incoordinate but recover facility as he gains strength. There are many geriatric illnesses that lead to permanent loss of coordination. When one suffers this deprivation (on either a temporary or continuing basis), walking becomes difficult or unachievable and manual tasks almost impossible.

The third weakness that becomes apparent is the loss of physical strength. As muscles lose their tonus and begin to atrophy, the individual finds his vitality and power diminishing. In most cases, dissipation is gradual and continues over a period of many years. It is far easier to compensate for loss of physical strength than for inability to coordinate or the slowing of reaction time.

There are, of course, other areas of debilitation which may be noticed. They tend to be unique, however, and will not be considered at this time. The three suggested above are the most frequent, obvious and significant and will invariably be found in the geronto sooner or later.

SLOWING DOWN OF MENTAL PROCESSES

As the individual moves into the gerontological period there seems to be, as a usual rule, a noticeable slowing down of the mental processes. With many, this slackening may be observed in middle maturity and become quite pronounced in later maturity. With those who age most facilely, however, impairment may be checked until the longevous years.

The first competency to suffer is normally the ability to memorize data. Many logical explanations of this particular loss have been suggested. The most acceptable concept to the developmentalist would be the belief that the older one gets the more information is already stored which could lead to conflict and give rise to the rejection of new facts. A second, rather logical suggestion indicates that the older one becomes the less strongly will he be motivated to accumulate data. If a significant use is indicated for new information the time required for memorization may be reduced by one-half. Significance, then, becomes a force that stimulates motivation. This principle would be readily accepted by the behaviorist. The most widely accepted cause is one that the writer considers untenable. This is the belief that there is a physiological deterioration of the brain cells that prevents memorization. This may well be true with the geriatric and senescent population but not with the *nonpathological aged*. Other suggestions not widely accepted will not, at the present time, be considered.

A second competency where loss is observed is in the comprehension of new ideas and the mastery of fresh concepts. Unique ideas may be difficult to accept because of the tremendous number of frames of reference through which the older person observes innovation. The young may identify as black or white the countless shades of gray the geronto views. To the young all things are good or bad; to the old none are either. A new idea which will be readily comprehended by a young adult may be incomprehensible to the older person since, through each frame of reference, a somewhat different evaluation may result. Only after a long period of reconciliation will the aged be able to comprehend a new idea and then, in all probability, his concept will be different from that of his son or daughter.

New concepts are difficult to master and for similar reasons. The older one becomes, the more concepts he will have identified and either accepted or rejected. Those that are adopted will become a part of one of the numerous hierarchies of ideas held by the individual. Each new presentation must be evaluated in terms of congruence and compatibility. Unrelated concepts (those neither in accord or in conflict with accepted opinion) may be mastered but *only* if there is need for something new and a strong motive for acceptance. Congruent and compatible concepts will be accepted if they tend to reinforce or expand existing dogma, tenets or precepts. Within this suggested framework, mastery of new concepts is not appreciably more difficult than in the younger years. Now, however, a reason for mastery must exist or the new concept will most certainly be rejected. Rejection and inability to master are two entirely different things!

It is often suggested that older people have difficulty reading given material. This is probably mere supposition and not based on valid experimentation. Here a definition of "reading" might be appropriate. If we define "reading" as an oral process and evaluate in terms of the ability to mouth sounds, we may truly find a difficulty. This problem is, however, only physiological and usually traceable to lost coordination. On the other hand, if we accept the far more logical definition, "the ability to obtain meaning from the printed page," we will probably determine that no impairment does obtain. Visual weakness frequently develops in the aged and may cause ineffectual reading despite the fact that the specific skill is unchanged. Here again the problem tends to be physiological and not due to the slowing down of the mental processes.

The geronto is, as a rule, considered to be unable to make decisions. Before age is accepted as the cause of this inability, one should determine if the given individual was able to make judgments *when he was young*. The writer should like to suggest that the percentage of the total population of youth and young adults unable to arrive at decisions is at least as great as the percentage of the nonpathological aged facing the same problem. Too many times we charge the gerontological population with weaknesses that are typical in other age groups as well. They may be more prevalent in the senescent and geriatric 10 per cent of the aged, but not among the 90 per cent of nonpathological elderly.

Before we accept as valid the concept that there is a true slowing down of mental processes, more longitudinal studies must be conducted. The writer would suggest that when such experimentation has been carried out it will be discovered that changes in the individual are minimal and that where they do exist they are due solely to pathological problems.

DEPENDENCE ON A RESTRICTED PATTERN OF INTERESTS

When the person is young and sampling life, he will have innumerable unrelated experiences. Each will be evaluated in terms of personal need or satisfaction produced and repeated or avoided in the future on the basis of determined merit. A majority of one's experiences may be integrated on a more or less temporary basis. During the rather long periods of adolescence and early maturity, those interests based on experiences that have continued to be satisfying tend to persist. Those that become less rewarding with maturity become lost.

Individuals during the period of middle maturity rarely develop significant numbers of new interests. In addition, many formerly compelling concerns lose meaning. As a result, when the individual approaches later maturity, his active interest pattern may have become quite narrow. This situation usually exists with all save that small percentage of truly creative persons. This group continues to search for new experiences and to persistently expand their engrossment.

When one becomes a member of the older generation, he may have such a narrow interest pattern that life loses purpose and becomes mere existence. The more intelligent, highly educated, well-adjusted segment of the population—especially those who have cultivated compelling hobbies—may escape this particular area of weakness.

INABILITY TO MAKE NEW AND NECESSARY ADJUSTMENT

One of the more frequently observed weaknesses of the older American is the inability to cope with a continuing series of compromises: compromise with self, with others, and with the environment.

The individual must learn to adjust to a changing self and to compensate for lost and spent faculties. By maximizing his residual talents and abilities, the compromise may not be too difficult. On the other hand, if he resists change and concession, the self frequently becomes intolerable and the individual, to survive, must identify with friends who may be able to bolster his faltering ego.

Adjustment to others may be simple or difficult. As a rule, harmonization with one's peer group is not impracticable. Differences tend to be minor and relatively easy to reconcile. With younger cliques the changed mores (or, if you prefer, folkways) may provide a disparity that is difficult to bridge. Here true compromise is necessary. Since members of the younger groups have much to lose and little to gain, the adjustment must generally be effected by the geronto. This is not impossible unless pride is too deeply involved.

Compromise with self and with others is only the first minor step towards adjustment. The older person must become reconciled to change of abode, of diet, of accepted worth, of financial independence and to countless modifications, substitutions and deviations that become mandatory with age.

The accumulated prejudices of a long life become well-entrenched and highly resistant to change or even modification. The bias and intolerance developed during the younger years may now so completely govern the individual self that any mutation of thought or belief is almost impossible. When the accumulated prejudices interact with the need to compromise and to adjust, the geronto faces a total problem almost impossible to reconcile. Frequently, professional assistance is necessary to assist in harmonizing the individual with his complete environment.

The person who in his younger and middle years learned to effect compromise whenever it seemed necessary and who was able to resist extensive and intensive development of bias and prejudice will become the most adequately adjusted geronto.

RESISTANCE TO COMPROMISE, CHANGE AND ENCROACHING DEPENDENCE

One who throughout a long life has been completely self-sufficient and independent may have many problems in learning to accept encroaching dependence. When others have always relied on an individual, it is most difficult for him to effect a reversal of roles. False pride tends to make this problem even more onerous. When the geronto is forced to admit his inabilities and to accept help from others he has assisted in the past, the ego undergoes a significant change. He loses his feeling of worth and often regards himself as a burden on others.

The older person frequently recognizes deteriorating abilities and skills but refuses to accept the loss as real and permanent. As a result, he rarely admits his present need to others, frequently because of pride in past accomplishments. Three categories of change must be faced as one moves into the longevous years: sociological, psychological and medical|. Requirements by areas vary from person to person. One may need no medical assistance but require much sociological and psychological help. Another may find only medical assistance necessary.

When a person has had a long and healthy existence without illness, it is difficult to accept dependence on medication as a new way of life. Feelings of inferiority may result and, on occasion, provide psychological problems which intensify the medical condition. If the individual can be led to a true understanding of his physical problems and an acceptance of a need that is quite normal, concomitant uncertainties may well be avoided.

Social compromise because of changing abilities will be averted if the individual can be convinced that *all change is not bad*. A new role may be more important even if not so glamorous as one formerly held. The advisory posture may be far more significant than the prestigeous active function once performed.

Compromise, change, compensation and adjustment in all of the various areas are closely interrelated. Maladjustment in one category will almost invariably lead to disharmony in others. All can be avoided by better developed understandings of self and one's true relationship to others. Pregerontological indoctrination should be provided to prepare individuals for the inevitable.

REDUCTION OF INDIVIDUAL MOTIVATION

There are two major types of motivation: physiological and sociological. The former is based on human needs, the latter on such powerful forces as desire for power, security, status, acclaim and companionship. Hedonistic motivation (achieving pleasure and avoiding pain, or winning rewards and escaping punishment) combines both physiological and social factors.

When one enters the gerontological period of life, many of the physiological forces become far less important. The sex drive is greatly reduced or may have completely disappeared and the need for food and for activity are diminished. More rest is required, elimination is a problem and homeostasis may become difficult to achieve.

The reduction in the force of the sociological motivators is even more significantly lessened. Need for power, prestige, adventure and companionship are reduced, but the exigency for praise probably remains undiminished. Hedonistic motivation is infrequently important. Of course, on an individual basis, any force may remain active into extreme old age.

There are many reasons for reduced level of motivation. After retirement there seems to remain with most people little desire to accomplish. Feeling that they have been discarded by society, they see no purpose for continuation in any active role. A second factor resulting from retirement is the removal of circumstances which will stimulate motivation. When opportunities are no longer available, impulsions are rarely generated. The older American may be temporarily motivated from time to time but the apparent fruitlessness of the activity leads to early extinction of the drive.

As one gets older, he usually finds that stress increases. This may be due to diminishing abilities and an increasing feeling of incompetence. The problems of aging themselves develop broad new stresses which, combined with the previously suggested increase in intensity, lead to many problems in adjustment. Among the numerous results of the strain of growing old may be the loss of any desire to live. Frequently, illness is difficult to overcome when the will to survive is no longer active. As friends and contemporaries disappear and the aged person continues to feel more alone and dependent on strangers, the drive to live is extinguished. This is, then, merely another evidence of loss of personal motivation.

If the geronto is to complete his productive, effective life, and truly "die with his boots on," it is essential that every effort be made to stimulate his motivation until the end.

REVERSAL OF PARENT-CHILD TO CHILD-PARENT RELATIONSHIP

One of the more difficult adjustments many older citizens are required to make concerns the reversal of relationships with others, especially their own sons and daughters. When the children were young, relationships were well-defined, lines of authoity rarely challenged and the several roles recognized and respected. The parent was the dominating force in the relationship, made all major decisions and served as guide, counselor and advocate.

Parent ─────────────────> Child

When middle adolescence is reached, some modifications in lines of authority and in the roles of both parent and offspring will be observed. The adolescent has achieved a new, partially reciprocal level in relationships precursive to maturity.

```
      ─────────────────>
Parent                    Adolescent
      <─────────────────
```

This interrelationship maintains in a state of flux until continuing modifications provide an eventual transition to the new reciprocal liason that will become a relatively stable relationship. There tends to be an equality in this new bond, but the senior member is usually considered, because of age and experience, the one to make final decisions.

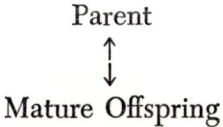

Parent
↑
↓
Mature Offspring

When the parent retires and enters the gerontological period of life, a new change may take place. A fresh reciprocal relationship tends to develop where the offspring rather than the parent makes the final decisions. This was not true when we had a patriarchal or matriarchal society, but in today's world, "age has been served" seems to be the accepted principle.

Offspring ——————————————> Parent
        <——————————————

The final change will usually take place when the parent enters the later longevous period and is no longer considered to be competent—competence determined by *age*, not by *performance!*

Offspring —————————————— Parent

These changes are difficult for the older person to accept. This is especially true if throughout his life he has possessed a dominating type of personality. With these individuals a cleavage may develop within the family which can even lead to complete rejection.

There are, of course, infinite numbers of additional weaknesses not considered here. Some will be individually important, others mere annoyances. The well-adjusted geronto may skip the major impairments, but it is doubtful if anyone will escape them all. Since this is true, attempts should be initiated to minimize the effects of those that cannot be avoided. If at the same time the many strengths that remain are maximized, the gerontological period will be certain to remain tolerable and may even become one of the most exciting periods of life.

Chapter Five

SOCIOPSYCHOLOGICAL CHANGE

FOLLOWING retirement many adjustments become necessary if the older person is to lead a happy, satisfied life. The problems, while evident to anyone who has studied the plight of the geronto, are not usually perceived by the general public. Even those individuals who determine the future of the senior citizens through legislation and by the development of programs to improve understandings, seem unaware of many facets of aging that are significant. All too often those who are charged with responsibility recognize only the obvious elements found among the stereotypic 10 per cent and remain oblivious to the issues affecting the nonpathological 90 per cent.

Sociopsychological change most frequently takes place *as a result of retirement.* As long as the older citizen remains actively employed in his profession, craft or business, or in a post-retirement substitute, changes will be minimal. The greater the involvement of the individual during his active years and the more happily he has been employed, the more difficult will be his adjustment to a life of imposed leisure.

DISENGAGEMENT

The process of disengagement is usually a painful course for one who has truly enjoyed his fruitful years. With the termination of his salaried occupation comes an ending of interaction with his colleagues. In addition, many attendant social relationships also cease. Even where contacts with former associates are continued, they are on a new and far less satisfying basis. New faces have replaced the retiree not only in his former positions but in attendant social functions as well.

The prestige that accrued to the individual through his profession or vocation gradually declines and may disappear completely. This is due not only to disassociation, but also to reduced social interaction and to change in the geronto's financial position. As his social position and financial condition change and his abilities tend to decline, there comes a reduction or ending of civic and community service for the geronto. As a rule, appointments to action committees are made from among those who are in a position to add prestige and distinction to the cause. The retiree may become a member of a work group which tends to remain anonymous or may be deleted from the roster of "willing workers."

When physical, mental and emotional change takes place, disengagement will be hastened. New attitudes and new interests which develop as concomitants of such change are frequently personal and nonsocial. When these attitudes and interests control the geronto's activities and his thinking, disengagement may be almost complete.

WITHDRAWAL

Withdrawal from society is the normal consequence of disengagement. There are two factors that play major roles in creating a climate for withdrawal: (1) feelings of inferiority and (2) reduced social motivation.

There are numerous elements involved in producing feelings of inferiority. None seem specifically related to aging per se, but all have their roots in retirement. Since this is true, withdrawal tends to take place following either voluntary or mandatory retirement regardless of the age of the individual. Mandatory separation from the ranks of the employed produces the more positive feelings of withdrawal while, in certain cases, voluntary retirement may fail to cause significant decampment.

With retirement, those gerontos who are unable to find new productive activities soon become members of the subculture of the aged. With this new affiliation, there develops a definite feeling of inferiority that becomes more and more pronounced as the individual accepts the reality of his new position in society.

The feelings of inferiority generally stem from a number of factors. The reduction of social and professional participation is the first and most important element. When one becomes an observer rather than an active contributor, his feeling of worth tends to disappear. Not only is this true, but a new personal disinterest becomes a strong contributing force in this withdrawal. With reduced activity and a deteriorating self-concept, the desire to be a functioning participant in business, professional and social activities is replaced with an acceptance of the role of beholder.

The changed self-concept becomes one of the most difficult problems with which to contend. It is insidious and is produced from both within and without. The external forces can be controlled but those that are produced within the individual remain adamant. Not only is the changed self-concept a major cause of feelings of inferiority, but it may also lead to reduced social motivation, another factor in producing withdrawal. The geronto finds himself less interested in a business and professional world that has changed drastically from the familiar scene he once knew. This disinterest also extends to a social world with which he no longer finds himself compatible. His one option seems to be a static affiliation with other social misfits in the new subculture.

In addition to personally reduced social motivation, there comes a very pronounced feeling of rejection which compounds the problem. With little personal interest and slight concern from society, it is inevitable that motivation to participate will be reduced to an almost nonexisent state.

The capstone of the problem will be found in the "It's too late now," syndrome. "Why bother, it's all over," becomes the philosophy of far too many of our older Americans. This syndrome is difficult to analyze and almost impossible to alleviate.

Only the well-educated, satisfactorily adjusted, economically secure will completely escape the problem of withdrawal. And, even with this small group, it may prove to be one of the major problems of aging.

Ecology is defined in the dictionary as the "biology dealing with the mutual relations between organisms and their environment." Here again we have a word with connotative implications that are far more inclusive than the limited dictionary meaning. Today, social, cultural, psychological and racial relationships are included with the biological in the total human ecological problem.

To the gerontologist, the social and psychological problems must receive prime consideration since these are the areas of greatest misunderstanding. Society in its many attempts to solve the problems of the senior citizens is merely compounding them. This comes not from malice, but rather from misunderstanding and an almost total lack of knowledge concerning the nonpathological geronto. As a usual rule, the *stereotypic* older person not only needs, but wants direct services. Such services are, in addition, all too frequently imposed on those who neither need nor desire them. As direct services are increased, opportunities to interact and to contribute are withdrawn. This action leads to the beginning of a changing social ecology.

During adult life, individuals average thirty hours per week in purely social interaction. This, over and above the interactive hours in professional, business and craft contacts, provides the active adult with an extensive, highly satisfying existence. In postretirement there is an abrupt cessation of contacts provided by employment. Following this comes a gradual reduction of social contacts until, during the gerontological period, they are reduced to ten or fewer hours each week. This change, while *normal* in our society, is *unnatural* as a way of life.

The tendency of society to ghettoize the old leads to an abnormal ecological condition. When we send those who are not senile to mental hospitals and sanatoriums, those who are not ill to nursing homes, and cajole the remaining gerontos to live in maturity centers and villages, we are creating an unnatural environment.

The natural social-ecological environment provides that all generations live not necessarily together but in close proximity to each other. When we remove the old, we leave the family group composed of infants, children, preadolescents and adults. The fact that the leavening influence of the geronto is now missing from the family group may possibly be one of the reasons for the disintegration of this important social unit.

The changed ecology which may prove unfortunate to the

family group is tragic to the oldster. Living with few contacts other than his age mates, his interests tend to remain with the past and his conversation primarily concerns his physical debility. A potentially productive life of ten, twenty, or even more years has, because of this ecological tragedy, ended on a sad note. It is time that society reconsider the problem of the older citizen.

When a man reaches the post-retirement years, he will find, as a usual rule, certain pressures exerted on him to reduce commitments and activities with which he has been involved. These pressures come from family and friends who want him to "enjoy the golden years" and from those who wish to replace him in those of his activities that produce status. Many gerontos willingly relinquish their commitments but certain types of retirees resist all pressures that are applied.

Those who are creative, imaginative and still vital may possibly increase their activities. This will be especially true where personal needs have not been completely satisfied and where motivation to serve and to accomplish remains strong. With the intelligent and educated individual, productive activities will possibly continue for many years and commitments may be increased because of added time made available through retirement.

For the individual having low-level abilities and inadequate education, any attempt to increase his activities and to accept new commitments will prove vain. No matter how strongly the inadequate older person may be motivated he will probably not achieve even a minimal level of success.

In many cases, new activities not previously available may present themselves. These will prove challenging to the creative oldster and provide him with opportunities to serve society. There are no true limits to the extent of activities available to the imaginative geronto who is adequately motivated. No amount of pressure from outside can prevent his continuing active life.

As we consider the various problems apparently caused by the aging process, we discover that in many instances, what was considered cause may have been in reality effect. The converse is also true and, as an example, retirement may well be a *cause* of sudden aging rather than the result. Many individuals retain their abilities, motivation, vitality and zeal until retirement becomes a fact. Without purpose, life becomes futile and the retiree immediately begins to age at a rapid rate.

The major problem of retirement may then be *not old age and retirement,* but rather the *transition* from adult to longevous responsibility. The individual is usually encouraged to accept a new professional and social role. Too often such a role holds little interest for the person who has been active and personally involved for many years. A great change in status tends to depreciate the self-concept and produce feelings of inferiority. Accompanying reduction of responsibilities becomes a contributing factor in this change and may lead to a feeling of age as a result rather than as a cause.

New sources of experience seem to be the most effective deterrents to aging. If the individual, in his post-retirement days, can develop fresh interests, innovative goals and modern concepts through new associations, hobbies and active participation in constructive endeavors, his chances of remaining "young" are increased and declining self-esteem may be prevented.

The presently accepted panacea for the elderly—direct services—inhibits continued development and accelerates the aging process. New programs which encourage "self-help" must be sponsored for the geronto, and encouragement provided for those who wish to continue in the mainstream of life.

In all probability the major trials and tribulations of retirement could be prevented by education. At least *ten* years before superannuation, employed persons must begin preparing for significant changes in their activities. A series of pre-retirement workshops should be provided to assist individuals in preparing for the future. There are four major and four minor areas where the writer believes preparation for change is probably most essential. The following should, then, be among the first items to be considered in any pre-retirement education program:

1. How to increase post-retirement income and how to live happily on a curtailed budget.

2. How to prevent deterioration of the self-concept and how to obtain maximum self-satisfaction from life.

3. Where to search for new areas of service available to the geronto. Service where personal satisfaction may be realized.

4. Developing hobbies and avocations, preferably ones that might become remunerative and lead to improved income.

5. Meal planning and cooking for the older person.

6. How to understand the problems of and adjust to sexual activities in the longevous years.

7. How to live with others in changing patterns of independence.

8. How to accept the rights of other to their own code of morality.

Countless other problems of retirement and of aging will be reported by older Americans that may well be considered in developing these workshops. The only ones who truly know the problems of the aged are the aged themselves. Their counsel should be considered in planning pre-retirement education.

SOCIAL ADJUSTMENT

Social adjustment is, in the final analysis, the most important item in sociopsychological change during the gerontological period. It is quite difficult to develop congruence between the required social behavior expected of the old and their inner compulsions, and between inner mental states and social expectations. Since society evaluates in terms of stereotypes (in almost every area of concern), *all* gerontos are expected to become like the stereotypic example and those who refuse to conform are considered abnormal.

The conflict, then, between society's perceptions of the aged and the aged themselves, and between the older person's perceptions of society and society as it truly exists, tends to be rather severe. There is a generally accepted belief that the old are a real threat to society because if they retain their powers and their resistance to change, youth will find few opportunities for advancement. Even greater is the fear that the old are a threat to necessary social change because of their tendency to become reactionary. At the same time, the aged perceive society as being a threat to their positions and to their ideas and ideals through imposed retirement and the tendency to relegate them to the new subculture of the aged. There is some justification for the fears in each camp. True understandings of each other would, however, reduce the tensions to a tolerable level.

The geronto is, as a general rule, quite resistant to social change. He has achieved a certain level of success and happiness in his world and sees no reason why anyone should wish to change such an acceptable climate. He has developed a fine hierarchy of prejudices and biased points of view that further inhibit change. In the major areas of social concern, the geronto is especially resistant. Schooled to accept segregation as a way of life, he will not and cannot accept the principles of integration. New patterns of behavior accepted by the younger generations and the changing mores become prime areas of conflict when concepts of what the geronto considers *basic morality* are violated. An especially controversial area of difference concerns foreign relations. The established concept that America must maintain the peace of the world is changing to an attitude of isolationism which is unacceptable to a majority of the older generation.

A careful appraisal of the attitudes of others seems mandatory if relationships between the generations are to be improved. Identification of specific points of conflict must be made and a search initiated for methods of reconciling the differences. In addition, some recognition of areas of agreement (and there are a great many) should serve to bridge at least a part of the "generation gap."

The gerontologist must recognize the importance of the changing social attitude toward the aged. Historically we have had, especially in the southern part of the United State, patriarchal and matriarchal rule. The senior member of the family was a minor diety who made all major decisions and exercised complete control over the clan. No one questioned the decisions of the head. In many respects the patriarchal/matriarchal rule resembled the order found in the Orient with its ancestor worship and reverence of the old—both within and without the family. The wisdom and the experience of the older person were considered invaluable and he was consulted in all areas of action.

Today, possibly because of the population balance, all this has changed. The control of resources has passed on to the middle-aged and the young adults. With the changing control of resources, decision-making has ceased to be considered a function of the old and has also passed to the younger groups. As a result, the old now share with the adolescents and preadolescents a feeling of insecurity, generally for the same reasons. To live in a society where your resources are *controlled for you* and *all decisions are made for you* even though you feel perfectly capable, becomes a source of annoyance.

While there are a great many reasons for this shift of control, education may be the more important factor. With past generations, the young depended upon their elders for much of their professional, business and craft knowledge. As a result, following a long apprenticeship, they developed a reverence for and dependence on the preceeding generation. Today the young tend to acquire their knowledge through formal education and, as a rule, bring new and possibly better ideas to their occupations. Since this is true, the young often feel superior to their elders, are not prone to accept guidance or advice, and strive not to complement but to replace their superiors.

The more complex our society becomes, the greater are the problems of gerontological adjustment. In simple societies *few* survived to old age. In pre-Christian days the average life span was less than thirty and among the pilgrims somewhat less than forty. Today, life expectancy has *almost doubled* and between 10 per cent and 12 per cent of the total population is over sixty-five. Every increase in percentage compounds the problem. Unless gerontologists are able to solve many of the pressing problems of the geronto, in another ten or twenty years life will be intolerable for an increasing number of people.

Traditional social institutions, churches, fraternal organizations and clubs of various types are not effective in the world of today. The young show little interest in any of these activities and are involving themselves in more personal types of recreation. The average age of members of church congregations advances by about two months each year. Fraternal organizations report declining memberships with initiations far below deaths and the young completely disinterested. Service and luncheon clubs have difficulty recruiting members form the younger segment of society and are supported, generally, by men in middle and late maturity. These institutions have in the past served to amalgamate the various generations into a cooperative society. As they lose their appeal and effectiveness, even greater cleavage between the ages may be expected.

The problems facing society in the very near future may prove to be obdurate. Unless the older citizens can be involved in a variety of activities they consider to be truly important, they may revolt against the establishment. What is presently a rather passive subculture may become an activist group of major importance. Several organizations are presently enrolling members on a national basis and certain of their leaders tend toward mild activism. The great mass of the gerontological population wants to remain a part of continuing society and has no desire whatsoever to become adversaries.

Part II
Changes in Psychological Function

Chapter Six

CHANGES IN SENSORY EXPERIENCE AND PERCEPTION

Ever since the first psychology laboratory was established in Leipzig by Wundt in 1879, experimentors have had a prime interest in sensory experience and the attendent perceptions. Traditionally, only five senses were recognized: sight, sound, taste, smell and tactile. The eye, stimulated by light waves, produces visual sensation; the ear stimulated by air waves, auditory experience. Vision and auditory sensation together with smell are frequently referred to as the "long-range" senses since they gather precise information about the environment from rather long distances. There are two other generic categories of senses: the somatic which includes pressure (touch) pain, cold and warmth, and the chemical which includes the olfactory, gustatory and one of the cutaneous reactions, slickness or oiliness. The tongue (primarily) receives stimulations from solubles with resultant gustatory sensations while the nose, stimulated by gaseous particles, produces olfactory impressions. The skin receives many types of stimulation—mechanical, thermal, electrical and chemical, to name a few—all producing cutaneous impressions. The organic actions developed by the above receptors produce vision, hearing, taste, smell and, with cutaneous experience, many reactions including pressure pain, heat and cold.

In recent years, several new senses included with the somatic have been recognized by psychologists. Among these are the kinesthetic, produced by a change of movement in muscles and joints; the organic, resulting from membrane and tissue stimulations in the alimentary canal and other organs; and equilibrium, stimulated by movement and muscle tension in the semicircular canal and in certain body movements. Kinesthetic sensation is produced by pressure; organic by hunger, thirst euphoria, etc.; and equilibrium by balance. Each sensation has two characteristics: quality and intensity. The quality and intensity of the sensation determines the perceptual level of the experience. In addition, the accuracy of the sensory impulse and the physical state of the responsible organ or organs will determine the preciseness of perception. Since this is true, the individual when tired, unwell, or influenced by spirits or drugs tends to be perceptually inaccurate. Does this same condition result from the aging process as well?

The experiences and values of the individual are other factors determining the logic and nature of the perception. For example, six men are standing on a hill observing a tranquil valley below. The grass is lush and a beautiful stream flows peacefully through the primitive landscape. Each of the six sees the *same* sight, but each has a different perception. The first, a real estate agent, visualizes a dwelling project for affluent individuals. The second, a fisherman, sees only the prospect of filling his creel. The third, a farmer, feels this to be the perfect spot for raising grain crops, while the fourth, a cattleman, sees the grazing potential. The fifth, an artist, recognizes the beauty of the spot while the sixth, a clergyman, says, "See what wonders God has wrought!" All have viewed the *same spot*, but each perceives it in the light of his background, experience and need. Accuracy of perception is evident in each evaluation, but attitudes change the perceptual value completely.

Throughout life there are continual changes in perception both in quality and quantity. Liminals and thresholds which vary from age to age, responses and changing values, together with added experience, contribute to perceptual modification.

Two examples of change are found in presbycusis and in presbyopia. With presbycusis the individual tends, at about age twenty-five, to begin to lose the ability to hear the higher frequencies. A very slow, but continuous, change may then be expected until at age sixty-five or seventy, the upper liminal may be only about 4,000 vibrations per second as compared to the 12,000 to 15,000 limit in youth. In addition, the difference threshold may change from 1 cycle per second (cps) to as great as 10 cps. A concomitant, which may be introduced at any age, reduces the sensitivity to changes in volume, resulting in the condition we usually refer to as deafness.

Presbyopia, produced by defective elasticity of the crystalline lens of the eye, leads to difficulty of accommodation and inability to attain a sharp focus. Since presbys means "old man," both presbyopia and presbycusis are usually considered conditions of the longevous periods.

All of man's faculties tend to become less functional in the older ages. Perceptual input (from stimulation received through the various sense organs) tends to decrease notably during the gerontological period of life. Not only the quantity but the quality of input as well decreases at a rapidly accelerating rate in the later longevous period. Very little research has been completed in the area of perception and aging. As a result, only empirical observations are presently available. While these may have some validity, a variety of experimental programs must be developed to provide objective data concerning perceptual loss.

Visual perception has probably been investigated in greater depth than any of the other areas. Ophthalmologists have rather good understanding of problems of vision and recognize the many causes of debilitation which they are capable of treating. Myopia, hyperopia, vertical and lateral imbalance and astigmatism are easily identified. Cataracts, glaucoma and other abnormal conditions of the eyes are rather well understood and preventive and correctional techniques are fairly adequate. No significant experimentation has, however, been completed in the area of change in color perception. Do individuals lose the capacity to distinguish between shades of color as they age? As one becomes older, he loses the ability to hear the higher frequencies of sound. Is there a comparable loss in responding to certain wavelengths producing color? Within the visible spectrum, wavelengths of 400 to 700 millimicrons are perceived by the average individual during young adulthood. One can usually distinguish more than 125 different steps. Since various wavelengths of the visible spectrum are typically perceived as producing diversified colors or shades of color, a change in difference threshold would alter an individuals' ability to discriminate accurately.

Light energy is turned by the eye into neural, electrical energy.

The presence of cones with three distinct pigments provides the basis for color vision. The different cones apparently have complex inputs to the higher levels of the brain that give rise to "opponent" cells. These cells are excited when the eye is stimulated by light at certain wavelengths and inhibited at other wavelengths. A fiber that is excited by wavelengths in the red region may be inhibited by those in the green region. Another opponent cell is excited by input from blue sensitive cones and inhibited by yellow. Visual responses to complex perceptual input determines the color sensitivity of the individual. What changes in color perception take place in the gerontological years? Are difference thresholds widened? Do liminals change? Do the cones deteriorate or do the neural pathways and the "opponent" cells become less functional? If there is a loss in color discrimination, is it a significant factor in the study of aging?

Empirically conceived answers to these questions are frequently suggested. The writer believes that objective data must be provided to gerontologists before adequate understandings of the aging process can be developed.

In the area of auditory perception, many hard facts have been provided through research conducted by physiologists and psychologists. As was mentioned earlier in this chapter, the loss of the ability to respond to the higher frequencies of sound (presbycusis) begins at about age twenty-five. Upper limits continue to drop until by age sixty, the liminal will range from 6.000 cps to 9,000 cps, and by age seventy possibly to 4,000 cps to 5,000 cps. Since fundamentals above 4,000 cps (the highest pitch on the piano) are infrequently found, these extreme frequencies are normally present only as "overtones" or "partials." These high frequencies, as components of lower pitches, determine the timbre or quality of tone. Here man's remarkable ability to compensate is well demonstrated. As he listens to music, his tonal memory colors the sounds he hears with frequencies to which he can no longer respond! Thus, *actual* loss does exist but *functional* response is unchanged.

Except in rare instances when physiological deterioration has progressed too far, prosthetic devices can correct *quantitative* but not *qualitative* loss in hearing. Volume of sound is measured by decibels (dB) and ranges from 0 dB (the lower liminal) to 130 dB (the normal upper liminal). A low whisper will measure 8 to 10 dB, while at 130 dB pain will be experienced. When one sustains excessive quantitative loss, normal conversation (about 60 dB) will possibly be inaudible and 140 dB—beyond the normal threshold pain—will become tolerable. The two aspects of auditory perception, quality and quantity, are rather well understood but their relationships to other debilitating factors has not been considered. Does each of the senses deteriorate at its own rate or is there a tendency for disintegration in one area to parallel that in others?

In hearing loss, does the debilitation take place in the receptors, the transducing of sound energy to neural energy or in the auditory cortex of the brain? Generally, we accept the premise that hearing loss in the old is due to deterioration of brain cells, to otosclerosis, which leads to the formation of new and inhibiting bone growth around the stapes, perforation of the eardrum and sensorineural impairment. While illness and accidents along with continual exposure to noise at the 120–140 dB level may produce premature impairment, most loss seems to be due primarily to the aging process.

Man's third major distance receptor is smell or olfaction; the sensitivity to odors, many of which emanate from some distance, is usually categorized as a chemical sense. This may be the single most important sense to many animals and insects, but in man it has decreased in effectiveness because of diminishing need and use.

Smell requires that certain molecules enter the nasal passages where the olfactory epithelium is located. Here are contained millions of hair cells each with 1,000 or more hairs per cell. These are reasoned to respond to the chemical properties of various stimulating agencies and are therefore classified as chemical receptors.

The axons of the hair cells, when stimulated by chemical agents, serve as transducers which change chemical to neural energy. These axons also become the olfactory nerves which transmit the neural impulses directly to the olfactory bulb of the brain. Since these receptors are accessible only to gases, substances must be volatile to be odorous. Man tends to respond only to organic substances. Little is known about why some substances are odorous and others are not, or why certain groups of odors smell alike. No stimulus key to the classification of odors has yet been successful. A recently proposed stereochemical theory of odor suggests that classification may depend on molecular shape.

We are all aware of the efficiency of the system to adapt to odors. Odors tend to disappear within a few minutes of exposure (even though the source of the stimulation remains constant) and, generally, the more concentrated the odor the more rapid the adaptation.

While a majority of the gerontos questioned by the writer testify that they have lost their sense of smell, no valid research can be found to document this supposition. If a loss does take place, is it due to disintegration of the receptors (the hair cells and hair in the epithelium), to the axons and/or the olfactory nerve, or to changes in the olfactory bulb of the brain? Since atrophy takes place in our bodies, it would seem logical to suggest that all of these mechanisms undergo debilitating change which would certainly modify olfactory perceptions. In addition, adaptation to *ever-present* odors may be so complete that the stimulation is no longer effective in producing sensations. This would seem a ripe field for the research psychologist working in cooperation with the gerontologist.

Gustatory sensations result from a combination of responses provided by the taste buds, modified by olfaction and kinesthetic cues from the muscles of the tongue and jaws. The dorsal surface of the tongue is dotted with taste buds in great numbers. In addition, papillae are found in the larynx, pharynx, palate, tonsils and epiglottis. These taste buds are constantly dying and being replaced. They are never, however, replaced quite as rapidly as they disintegrate. As a result, from childhood to old age there is a continuous (even though slight) change in taste sensation which leads to a final, almost complete loss in extreme old age. As in all areas of debilitation, the rate of loss varies greatly. As a consequence, some lose this sense in early years while others maintain satisfactory functioning to rather old ages. Smoking, excessive use of alcohol and continued irritation will accelerate this loss.

Taste buds are chemical receptors and respond to only four elemental qualities of taste: sweet, sour, bitter and saline. Sour-sensitive spots are located along the sides of the tongue, sweet-sensitive along the tip, bitter-sensitive spots at the base and salt-sensitive spots on the tip and sides. Many substances activate two types of receptors each of which responds in the characteristic fashion rather than in a modified manner.

What we "taste" in food is determined by the ratios established between the responses of the various taste buds, and is greatly modified by smell, by sensations of warmth (or cold) and by cutaneous and kinesthetic impressions. Texture may prove a highly integral part of the total response while many spices and certain acid and "hot" foods provide cutaneous sensation. All of these stimulating factors become a part of a hierarchy of sensations which provide a total experience. As with several of the other senses, contrast may determine specific responses. If one is eating cake or candy, lemonade tastes sour. A bite of pickle, by contrast, will make the same lemonade seem sweet.

When individuals move into the period of later maturity, the sensations of taste become less intense. By the time they reach the later longevous period, they usually maintain that they have lost all sense of taste. How much of this loss is physiological and how much is psychological needs to be determined. One factor that might possibly be considered is the bland diet frequently given the old. Could this possibly be responsible for the reported lack of flavor? Would it have been just as tasteless at age twenty? Would pizza, spice cake, chili or hamburger seem bland to the old? If this is true loss, which factors deteriorate first? The actual sensation from the taste buds? The olfactory overtones? The cutaneous and kinesthetic components? This could well become an area of importance to be investigated in depth by the gerontological psychologist.

There are many different types of cutaneous sensations, e.g. pressure change, warmth, cold, pain and the oleaginous response (which may be considered one of the chemical sensations). The thin outer layer of the skin (the epidermis) is composed of dead cells and contains neither blood vessels nor nerve fibers. Its primary function is a protective one, despite the fact that many free nerve endings innervate the *under portion* of the epidermis. The dermis is replete with nerve endings, blood vessels and cutaneous receptors. The function of the free nerve endings (found also in small number in the epidermis) is probably related primarily to pain.

Exploration of the skin surface with tiny hammers and fine wire probes reveals a pattern of pressure-sensitive spots. These spots represent points of high sensitivity to a pressure gradient. We tend to be more sensitive to changes than to constant pressure. As a result, the wearing of clothing is not something of which we are continually aware. Various parts of the body respond to pressure at different levels with the threshold lowest in the tongue, lips and the tips of the fingers.

When we touch the body with stimulators at skin temperature (usually about 32° c.,) no thermal sensation is apparent. Rising temperatures produce a sensation of warmth while lower ones stimulate cold receptors. Generally, in a square centimeter of the skin will be found about six cold spots, but only one or two warm ones. We usually accept the premise that there are individualized receptors for heat and cold rather than one type responding in direction only. One reason we believe this is that when a cold spot is identified as such it yields a sensation of cold even if stimulated by heat. Little is known about the nature of the receptors of cold and heat or the transmission of sensation to the consciousness. Adaptation is rather rapid, within ranges of safe tolerances, and sensation received from sources may depend on whether they are absorbent, e.g. cloth, or reflective, e.g. metals. Here again, contrast is a factor in sensation. If one has been in the hot sun, a warm bath feels cold while after exposure to cold, cool water feels warm.

The old tend to believe that they have increased tolerance—even need—for heat and that they cannot withstand any degree of cold. As a result many migrate to warm climates when they enter the gerontological period of life. House temperatures are frequently kept so high that younger individuals feel uncomfortable when the old are at ease.

While little is known concerning the transmission of temperature stimulation to the consciousness, it seems logical to suggest that debilitation of the body may lead to significant changes. Here again, we find a fertile field for experimentation. It is doubtful if any method of inhibiting debilitation can be discovered, but tolerances might be increased in the old.

Pain is associated with more than just the skin. Little is known, however, about pain from within except that it tends to be deep, dull and even more unpleasant than the sharp localized pain on the body surface. Many types of stimuli—punctures, scratches, heat, cold and others—may produce pain.

Evidence points to the free nerve endings present in the under portion of the epidermis as well as in the dermis as the receptors for cutaneous pain. Evidently, injury to the tissue involves injury to the nerve fibers themselves. This is verified by the fact that some spots on the skin, when punctured by a needle, produce no pain. We do not know what portion of the brain mediates pain or just how the sensation is transduced. Measurement of pain is difficult due to problems of stimulus, subject resistance and variable tolerances. Sensitivity to pain is often absent due to neurotic reactions or possibly hypnosis or autohypnosis.

That each of the cutaneous sensations is unique in itself seems to be proven by the fact that specific responses may be produced by diverse types of stimulation. Heat or cold applied to pain receptors produces pain, a prick of a cold or heat receptor induces a sensation of cold or heat and pressure may produce any response. While all receptors perform independently, we tend to respond largely to total stimulation of the organism. As a result, in normal situations we tend to receive composite impressions with specific overtones.

The receptors which produce kinesthetic sensation are located in the muscles, tendons and joints of the body. When the parts of the body move, these receptors are stimulated by stretch and pressure which gives rise to kinesthesis. This sense is important in the determining and controlling of body position and movement. Actually, much of what we call "touch" involves the kinesthetic sense, especially in areas where chemical reactions are not present. This sense plays a major role in maintaining an erect posture, walking, talking and in the performance of a variety of motor skills.

There are two somatosensory areas of the brain, the primary and the secondary. When there is damage to these parts of the brain either by accident or through illness, there is a distinct loss of the cutaneous and kinesthetic senses. The individual as he becomes older is far more susceptible to illness, to accident and to atrophy of the kinesthetic sensory systems. While aging is not the primary cause, it may well be a contributing factor.

Every individual is aware of deviations in body position even when the change is not a result of conscious effort. The receptors involved in this experience are found in the labyrinth or inner ear. Within the labyrinth are the three loops extending in three different planes that make up the labyrinthine or vestibular receptors. The function of these receptors is to keep one informed of his position in space and direction of movement up, down, left, right, backward or forward. The semicircular canals contain liquid which activates the hair cells that form the true sense receptors. In addition, two saclike chambers in the vestibule at the base of the canals (the saccule and utricle) respond to gravity and straight-line motion.

The function of this sense seems to be related to need to maintain equilibrium. Many physiological stimuli produce motion sickness which leads to nausea and a variety of incongruous sets of sensations. A conscious effort is required to maintain equilibrium which is signaled by labyrinthine sensations. Were it not for these sensations, one would frequently be subject to accidents due to faulty body position. The hair cells in the semicircular canals are activated by the movement of the liquid and transmit nerve impulses to the cerebral cortex and to the thalamus where feelings of pleasure or discomfort are controlled.

As one moves into the gerontological period of life, these receptors become more important and probably less functional. Many of the accidents of the old and much of their discomfort may be traced to debilitation of this particular sense.

All of man's faculties tend to become less functional at older ages. Since this is true, the geronto must learn to compensate for loss if he expects to live a happy normal existence.

We have ample evidence to prove that man does compensate for changing perceptions produced by diminished sensory experience. Much of the compensation comes from his memory and imagery which tends to fill in sensory loss. Thus, even though true sensation is diminished, the stimulation to perception may remain fairly constant. All compensation, however, cannot be credited to memory and imagery. The theory of extrasensory perception (ESP) as projected by J. B. Rhine would explain much of the perceptual strength of the older person. The writer should like to suggest, however, that stimulation does not come from *without* man's perceptions, but through the functioning of perceptual tools not yet recognized and identified. The kinesthetic, organic and equilibric senses have been generally accepted only in the last twenty years. Prior to that time, the five cardinal senses alone were considered. Too many bits of evidence presently exist to categorically state that unidentified perceptual tools do not exist. Psychologists who tend to ridicule ESP should search for identifiable new senses to explain the many observed phenomena which are not results of any known sensory stimulation.

The writer should like to suggest that these unidentified senses may increase as individuals move into the longevous period. This increase could possibly compensate for the measurable decline in sight, sound, taste, smell and tactile reactions that cannot be credited to memory and imagery.

Chapter Seven

CHANGES IN MOTIVATION

WHY are some individuals continually impelled to achieve and accomplish while others have no apparent desire to succeed? One, and quite possibly the only answer, lies in the continuing motivation of individual behavior as based on one or more of the accepted theories or on forces as yet unidentified. There are at least six concepts of motivation which are presently, or have been in the past, accepted as valid. All theories can probably be categorized under one of three generic classifications: physiological, psychosocial and ego-integrative.

Physiological (sometimes called biological) motivation is derived from human needs and wants. Among the true needs (those factors necessary to life itself) are food, water, air, elimination, homeostasis, rest and activity. Without any one of these, death would result. Thus, the need for each of these provides high-level motivated behavior. Individuals frequently kill to satisfy their human needs. Among the physiological *wants* are sex and stimulation. These are *not needs* since the organism can exist (though not too happily) without satisfaction of mere wants. Despite the fact that there is a true difference between needs and wants, they are almost equally important as motivational forces. This would seem to indicate that learned appetites may become just as compelling as basic organic needs. While it is true that human wants have their roots in physiological mechanisms just as do needs, the compulsion to satisfy comes from experience and pleasurable reactions. With sex, as an example, primary excitation in the male may be traced to testosterone and in the female to estrogens (without these hormones little sexual desire can be aroused) but their motivational strength is negligible until learning and experience have been introduced. It would seem then that hedonistic overtones may play a part in creating compelling wants.

The relative strengths of the biological drives are continually shifting. At different periods of life, wants and needs are modified by physiological change. When one is young, activity is paramount; in old age, rest tends to be more necessary. A concomitant of this change may be a reduction in need for food and/or water. A gradual shift or modification of the drives rather than abrupt change is more frequently observed. Elimination is directly related to input and, as a consequence, modifies in an almost parallel manner. As the individual's metabolic rate varies, the *need* for oxygen changes in almost direct ratio. An important element in homeostasis is body temperature control. A complex mechanism balances heat loss against heat production. Changes in this balance occur in aging and, as a result, the need for warmth may become an important drive.

The regulatory function in all of the physiological drives is apparently found in the reticular formation and its dominance of the hypothalamus. The precise manner in which this portion of the brain functions has not as yet been determined. It seems to mediate all pleasure, pain and quality of function and to transmit instructions to the concerned organs to correct performance errors. We find here another comprehensive area for the experimentalist and the gerontologist. Answers to many of the questions concerning modifications of physiological motivation might serve to make old age a happier period of life.

The second generic classification, the psychosocial, includes such powerful forces as the desire for power, security, prestige (status), praise, companionship (affiliation) and adventure. Curiosity, deference, order, exhibition, autonomy, succorance, dominance, abasement, nurturance, change and aggression are other forces in the psychosocial category.

To the average person, the five most frequently admitted social motives are needs for security, affiliation, praise, achievement and power. In rank order of importance there will be considerable variation. Many individuals will substitute one or two of the other motives, but almost everyone will include at least three from the five listed above.

These are all considered in this presentation as psychosocial despite the fact that they are frequently viewed only as social. The writer believes that the true motivating force is psychological, even though the cue to motivation may be social. Without the psychological to provide the drive, the social implications would be merely academic.

Certain motives in this generic classification are apparently inborn or learned without formal training. These are found in many animals, especially the primates, as well as in human beings. Curiosity, the need to investigate, is one of the fine examples of inborn motives. Others in this category may be exhibition, affiliation, succorance, dominance and aggression. Many of these are found in higher degree among animals than men. When they become important to a man, however, they may, through learning, become dominant out of all proportion.

Members of several subcultures, particularly hippies, activists and drug devotees, may disavow power, prestige, achievement and praise, together with deference, order and dominance as *motives of the establishment*. They are inclined to list as most important adventure, succorance, affiliation, curiosity and abasement.

Members of ethnic subcultures who resist integration into total society frequently develop completely different hierarchies of motivating forces. This will be due, in the main, to their unique concepts of good and bad and divergent life goals. Each person, regardless of his cultural heritage, will develop that hierarchy of motivating forces needed to achieve his individual life goals. As certain targets are attained, they may become motives to lead to new achievements. Only in rare cases will fulfillment of desired ends serve to stifle total motivation.

Ego-integrative motivation is based on certain drives which are important to the development of a normal, effective life. These factors have little relationship to psychosocial or physiological motivation and are infrequently considered by authorities in the field. If we hope to develop fairly complete understandings of *individual* behavior, however, we must determine how well-integrated the subject's personality seems to be. All other motivation may be modified and delimited by these individual factors.

Among the elements to be considered in an evaluation of ego-integrative motivation are such constituents as need for contact with reality, harmonious reactions to reality, increasing self-direction and acceptable balance between success and failure, attainment of maturity at one's level of development and adequate conceptual abilities.

In many respects, ego-integrative motivation is reminiscent of the phenomenological approach where *all* human behavior is motivated by the need to maintain and enhance self. The writer hesitates to accept the phenomenological approach in its totality because of certain limiting factors, e.g. the need to partially distort some motivating forces to bring them into proper context. It seems that a three-category system (physical, psychosocial, ego-integrative) provides better total understandings of theories of motivation.

Many authorities list among motivational categories the hedonistic. This may well be a separate classification, but on the other hand, could be considered a concomitant of numerous forces in all categories. The desire to achieve pleasure and to avoid pain tends to be a part of any physiologically motivated behavior. By the same token, an added force in all psychosocial motivation is the desire to obtain rewards and to escape punishment. Hedonistic overtones may also be observed in ego-integrative forces but probably not to an equal degree.

Many of the ancient Greek philosophers would have considered hedonism the one master motive to total behavior. Today it may be viewed as a major drive by many; to this writer, it is merely an important force in determining the intensity of more frequently accepted basic motives.

A goal achieved by one drive may become a new motive to satisfy some particular additional requirement. In many cases the progress motive-goal-motive-goal-motive-goal may become almost a chain reaction leading to the development of complex behavioral patterns. In the motivational change cycle, a physiological drive may achieve a goal which becomes a psychosocial motive to achieve another ambition. Motives among the many categories are, then, mutually inclusive rather than mutually exclusive. Each individual during his mature years tends to remain highly motivated. The nature of individual motivation will vary greatly from person to person with no two supporting the same identical hierarchy. Differences in behavior patterns are directly related to individual motivation.

During the early longevous period (starting at around age 68) a noticeable decrease in motivational compulsion is observed. Many drives disappear completely while others are merely reduced in intensity until they become ineffectual. This is frequently charged to aging but, in the opinion of the writer, is more probably a part of the retirement syndrome. As long as one is actively engaged in useful pursuits, either vocational or avocational in nature, motivational level may remain effectual. When, on the other hand, the person is completely relegated to the discard, no reason remains for activity and drives deteriorate.

During the productive years, the peer group gives support and encouragement to its members. Motives are reinforced by consensus and status is enhanced by accomplishment. After retirement the individual, without reinforcement from others, not only feels a loss of status but experiences a gradual decline of motivational vigor in all categories. The withdrawal of reinforcement may be one key to the loss of incentive that is usually considered inevitable in aging. Possibly a program to provide peer reinforcement may be one of the keys to minimizing the importance of the retirement syndrome.

Extrinsic motivation, where incentive comes from outside sources, will disappear rather abruptly while intrinsic, which comes from physiological or ego-integrational forces, will slowly diminish until it dissipates. As long as goal-directed activity provides satisfaction it will never completely disappear.

Changes in Motivation

After retirement, one's perceptions of his role in life will alter. The need to maintain self in that role then changes, diminishes, disappears. This leads to negative modification of the self-concept and serves as a brake to motivational drive.

One explanation of physiological motivation is suggested by S-R bond psychologists. They maintain that behavior is a result of certain stimuli activating the various receptors of the organism. When the organism is activated, certain predictable responses will result. While it is possible that certain psychosocial responses may be activated by a controlled stimulus, basically such responses tend to be physiological. With this theory conscious, subconscious and unconscious factors tend to be disregarded. While this assumption is an oversimplification, it does provide us with a point of departure in considering observable changes in motivation during the older ages. A decline in the functional qualities of the organism will provide weakened responses to stimulation. While motivation may remain as strong as during the younger years, the diminished response may be wrongly credited to ineffectual stimulation.

The physiological needs and wants change significantly in the later longevous period. Activity becomes less necessary and sleep and rest moreso. As activity declines, need for food decreases while thirst may remain constant. Homeostasis is far more difficult to achieve due to alterations in physiological condition. The sex drive tends to reduce as hormonal output decreases. It never completely disappears and can be increased by the administration of hormone injections.

Frequently a drive may become unimportant because the goal which has been achieved completely satisfies need. When this takes place, the motive will cease to exist. For example an indivual has been strongly motivated in youth and maturity to achieve security. In old age he may have attained this goal completely, in which case, the drive may disappear.

In summation, we may say that alterations in motivation are readily observable during the longevous years. Among the many reasons for these changes we find the following:

1. Loss of peer reinforcement.
2. Complete satisfaction of need in an area.
3. Change of role.
4. Changing self-concept.
5. Physiological debilitation.
6. Ego satisfaction.
7. Ego-integrative fulfillment.

As we study the total behavior of the old, we must consider motivational change as a possible factor in determining individual aging processes. Almost every human function depends to some degree on strength of motivation. In many cases functional change *does not* exist but because of little motivation appears to be greatly impaired. This is an important area in gerontology and merits continuing investigation.

Chapter Eight

AWARENESS IN THE GERONTOLOGICAL PERIOD

AS WE attempt to evaluate the changes in awareness that take place in the older population, we find many variables. Awareness is not a function in itself, but rather an interaction between self and the environment. Since this is true, it becomes a completely individual matter not subject to categorization.

It has frequently been suggested that among the faculties lost or diminished during older ages is awareness. This is another of the many fallacious concepts that exist in our appraisal of aging. Since awareness is *not* a faculty but an interaction between many faculties and continually changing environments, evaluation becomes a highly complex and individualized process. Thus, any categorical assessment of changes in levels of awareness must have questionable validity.

Direct impressions received through our senses produce perceptual experience. We may, however, taste, smell, hear, see and feel *without any conscious response.* Impressions may remain dormant and possibly, at a later date, impinge on consciousness. The key to conscious experience is awareness. Since awareness is not a function in itself, it must be considered an interaction, a state of freedom from inhibiting forces or a favorable climate for response. When one is ill, tired or under the influence of alcohol or drugs, a favorable climate for perceptual experience is not present. Either no reaction will be noted or the response will be invalid and distorted. When one is concentrating on other matters or surrounded by noise or distractions, the sense impressions may be stored for later retrieval or fail to impress completely. Interaction between the stimulus, other stimuli and the environment is absolutely necessary to valid response. This is awareness —the key to perceptual effectiveness.

When one enters the gerontological period of life, changes in awareness may become more noticeable. Even a superficial evaluation will indicate significant change. The important question seems to be not is there *change* in awareness, but rather, is there a true *loss?* Change is probably inevitable—it has been taking place throughout life—but can change necessarily be considered loss? Awareness should probably be equated with personal need. Is awareness of the insignificant, the valueless, the unrelated in the environment mandatory? It would seem that our concern should be largely with potential functional awareness rather than with the observable.

The sensory system is selective. We tend to see, hear, smell, taste and respond to desired stimuli. While many may be in a room, we frequently see only one or two. We tune in and tune out voices and sounds almost at will. We listen only to selected conversations and can shift our attentions from one to another at will. The cellist tends to hear the cello in the orchestra predominately while no one but the bassist consciously hears the basses. We see certain colors most clearly because of personal selection and smell those odors we either like or dislike. The two classes of simuli to which we respond most readily are those we enjoy and those that annoy. We tend to ignore those to which we are indifferent. This control of selectivity may be either conscious or unconscious. Certain stimuli may impinge on our consciousness despite our efforts to filter them out. The older we get, however, the more selective our perceptions tend to become. This may be, at least partially, controlled by changes in awareness and the new realization that *many things are not important.* Control of involuntary responses may give an impression of loss that is erroneous.

What we see is really a complex brain process, not, as is commonly believed, merely registration of an image produced by our sensory system. Our experiences and conceptions temper the purely sensory impressions resulting in a truly gestalt response. Those things we hear are equally complex. In every sound—speech, music, noise—we hear the fundamental and a wide range of partials (overtones). When, as we get older, presbycusis inevitably reduces the functional ability to hear the higher frequencies, *our remembered responses replace the true response and we hear the sound as it actually is!* Awareness requires a stimulus but not necessarily a complete stimulus. Not only the *present* environment but *past* environments as well interact with the self and produce a true level of awareness, psychologically, that may be functionally impossible. In all areas of perception, memories from the past serve to enhance the present and help us to maintain relatively high performance levels. Since this is true, those individuals who had high levels of awareness in their peak years will probably have high levels in the gerontological period.

Sensory isolation provides an environment that may significantly reduce awareness. When few fresh stimuli are provided and the individual must rely on memory and vicarious experience alone, even compensation is almost impossible. Continued, unvaried repetition of identical stimuli may also cause awareness to disappear. As an example, are you aware of the articles in a room in which you spend a great amount of time? If you live by a busy highway or a railroad track, do you hear the cars or trains? If you live near a feedlot, do you smell the ever-present effluvia? The visitor to Colorado sees the beauty of the mountains that the *average* resident fails to see.

Normal awareness is probably an interlayering of numerous experiences from the past, the present, and the vicarious, blended with effective stimuli. The individual, then, who is most aware is that person who has had the widest range of perceptual experience throughout life, heightened with imagination and curiosity to stimulate awareness.

Drugs frequently produce alterations in awareness. The same effect may be produced by intensive meditation (yoga, Zen, etc.). Since these are not (at least not as yet!) the norm, they need receive only passing mention.

If we evaluate only the geriatric and senescent aged, we will certainly find a high level of loss of awareness. On the other hand, if we examine the nonpathological aged populations we will probably find little change from that found in the mature years.

Decreased levels of awareness are *not a result of age* but, rather, of a variety of pathological conditions. Even the young and the mature populations lose their awareness when ill and/or mentally incapacitated.

It would seem, then, that the loss of awareness attributed to aging is the result of other factors present only in that stereotype accepted as the *normal* old person. This despite the fact that only 10 per cent of the gerontos in our population embody the characteristics found in this rather small sample.

Chapter Nine

SHORT-TERM AND LONG-TERM MEMORY

MANY psychologists believe that there is a fundamental difference between short-term and long-term memory while an almost equal number maintain that no disparity exists. As one might well expect, experimental evidence exists supporting both sides of the controversy. Those who argue against a difference suggest that short-term memory is that kind one has after only one trial while long-term is produced after several. They also contend that the same kinds of things interfere with both types of memory. The only difference, then, lies in the degree of original learning. Argument for a theoretical difference suggests that it takes a few seconds for a trial to consolidate and that memories for unessential stimuli and events are infrequently put into the permanent record. Categorization almost invariably exists in long-term, but rarely in short-term memory. In addition, long-term tends to be more closely related to the individual's reaction patterns and tropisms. This writer believes that more evidence exists favoring a difference. As a consequence, the following presentation is based on this belief.

Short-term memory is closely related to perception and to awareness. It is primarily produced by contact with the environment. Even the briefest stimulus may produce a perceptual trace which will continue for a short time. In the act of perceiving, one is able to respond to only a limited sample of stimuli at any one time. If only four or five are to be reported, responses are, usually, rather accurate. If, however, more than ten are presented, only six or seven will be retained in a majority of cases. How long each will remain recallable will depend largely on the utility and pertinence of the information and the individual motivation to retain. When information is categorized, it will be retained for longer periods of time than if treated as unrelated bits of data.

Short-term memory is valuable solely when need is temporary and *retention might become an annoyance.*

If we were to attempt a scientific study of memory, it would be necessary to control and measure at least four variables: (1) what was learned, (2) how well it was learned, (3) how long ago it was learned and (4) the degree of personal satisfaction realized from the perceptual experience. In such a study, *what was learned* would need to be evaluated in terms of its meaningfulness and utility at the time of learning and of its continued significance and usefulness. *How well it was learned* would require an understanding of the level of motivation and the number of repetitions that accompanied the learning. *The degree of personal satisfaction realized* would be determined by evaluating the individual's hedonistic nature. *How long ago it was learned* would provide an evaluation of the innate retentiveness of the subject's mind.

A wide variety of hypotheses have been suggested in an attempt to relate long-term memory to certain biochemical changes. The most recent speculations have proposed primary modifications in ribonucleic acid (RNA) and deoxyribonucleic acid (DNA) molecules. One suggestion assumed the passage of a specific pattern of bioelectrical changes in the RNA molecules. These molecules direct the synthesis of new proteins which dissociate selectively. The resultant action causes the release of transmitter substances at the synapse when the original bioelectrical pattern of stimuli recurs. With this concept, memory might be postulated to be largely, if not entirely, physiological. Repeated stimulation would most certainly increase the probability of synaptic transmission. Much additional documentation is needed to substantiate this exciting new concept. It does, however, provide a unique hypothesis. This is only one of numerous theories advanced by psychologists to explain the phenomenon of long-term memory. It is presented here primarily to serve as a contrasting theory almost diametrically opposed to one the writer wishes to introduce for consideration.

Short-term and long-term memory are both closely related to information storage and retrieval. In short-term memory, a relatively small number of items (possibly 6 or 8) may be stored at any one time for almost instantaneous retrieval. With long-term memory, an entirely different situation exists. Recall is not immediate, but delayed. Information tends to be stored by categories rather than by individual items and some sorting-out process is necessary to provide specifics. Apparently no true limit exists that will restrict the number of items which may be stored for long-term recall nor the length of time each will remain available. There is, in fact, evidence to indicate that long-term items are *never* forgotten. They may remain for many years in the conscious where almost immediate retrieval is possible. Eventually, those items that are not utilized will shift to the subconscious. Recall now becomes somewhat more difficult. Associative techniques may be used by the individual to bring these items into current focus. In extreme situations psychoanalysis or a similar type of psychotherapy may be required to effect retrieval.

Imagery plays an indispensable role in information storage. Thus, the person with the greater potential for true imagery will tend to be the individual with the finest memory. Dr. Carl E. Seashore, during his early years as a general psychologist, proposed an evaluative self-rating scale for determining personal imagery. Each of the items was recorded on a five-point scale ranging from "completely" to "not at all." Items from this test included the following samples:

Recall the smell of a rose.
Remember the sound of a piccolo playing a high note.
Imagine the taste of a bit of steak.
Recall the smell of an onion.
Remember the feel of a swatch of velvet.

If one can recall the smell of a rose as completely as though he were holding one, can remember perfectly the timbre of the piccolo, the feel of the velvet, the taste of steak and the smell of onion, his imagery is perfect. If no recall takes place, imagery is nonexistent. Some individuals have excellent all-inclusive imagery, while others experience little if any recall. This might be used as a device to determine the potential long-term memory of the person.

With short-term memory, the perceptual impression need not

be strong nor lasting, but must have little interference. One remembers a telephone number long enough to dial, if some other stimulus does not interfere. Even a minor perceptual input may completely destroy this very short-term item. Here imagery is of negligible value since use extinguishes the memory. If extinction does not take place, the memory becomes glutted with perceptual images of minimal value. Since this is true, *forgetting* is equally as important as *remembering*. Short-term memory is purely utilitarian. When an item is not longer pertinent, it must be extinguished.

Strangely, there seems to be little if any relationship between intelligence and memory. The writer once knew a fifteen-year-old retarded boy who knew the telephone number, the post office box number and the auto license number of all of the residents of a town with a population of 3500 people. This boy, however, when helping his mother in her small store was unable to make change for a quarter. Memory per se, either short-term or long-term, is of little value without at least a minimum of utility. The individual with a great store of memorized information may become highly erudite but cannot, unless the information has specific use, be considered an educated person.

It is generally accepted that the normal young child possesses a rather high level of eidetic imagery. As the youngster becomes educated, there seems to be a decreasing need for eidetics. Since this is true, the faculty disappears from nonuse. A residue of imagery does, however, remain to most individuals though the eidetic quality probably disappears. This residue serves as a stimulant to perceptual memory. Those perceptual experiences tend to remain fairly constant throughout the life span. Interestingly, the pleasant and beautiful tend to stimulate imagery more than do the painful and drab. It has frequently been said that could a woman remember the pains of chiildbirth, there would be no families larger than three! Still, with a conscious effort, complete recall of almost any experience should be possible.

There are countless degrees of imagery. Some develop high-level abilities in visual areas and lower plateaus in auditory. Generally, however, higher attainments in one area indicate potential at least in all. Through the use of one's total abilities in imagery, long-term memory potential may be realized. Not all authorities agree as to the importance of imagery in memory development. The numerous "memory training courses" that have been sold to the gullible through the years were usually developed through mnemonics. Until recently this was a dirty word to psychologists. In recent years, however, even the purist is accepting certain *gimmicks* as having value. Noncognitive memory is probably impossible through imagery but becomes simple by using mnemonic associations. Any methods that makes it possible for an individual to develop his long-term memory must be good. If it works, use it.

It is generally accepted as fact that there are significant changes in memory as one passes the middle years. As far as the writer has been able to determine, however, no significant experimentation exists to document this supposition. Too many of the "facts" concerning the aged are based on insufficient information to have even a minimum level of validity.

Observation of, and desultory conversation with the aged, leads one to believe that long-term memory remains excellent, but that short-term seems almost nonexistent. The geronto remembers his youth with clarity but does not recall what he had for breakfast or his present address and telephone number. He remembers his mother's smile and his father's woodshed but forgets his doctor's orders. If memory is physiological, why does the old persist and not the new? If his mental faculties are declining, how do old memories persist while new ones fail to impress? It would seem apparent that changes in memory are probably not traceable to old age per se. Several suggestions which may explain the apparent paradox seem pertinent.

The older memories are based on experiences provided during the years when perceptual abilities were at their very peak. Regardless of what memory theory one subscribes to, intensity of perceptual input tends to determine effectiveness of impression. As a result, memories from the past are usually based on strong input while those of the present depend on current perceptual levels. One may well say that when an individual's perceptual abilities decline, memory that must then be based on diminished input will be less effective. This could possibly explain the poor short-term memory of those whose perceptual abilities have declined significantly.

A second element that could prove a causative factor in short-term loss might be the level of motivation. In all too many cases, the geronto faced with what appears to be a pointless future loses the stimulation of his motivation. Since this tends to be true, few things seem significant enough to impress. Were it possible to increase the older persons motivation together with his feelings of the "importance of things," his short-term memory might become equal to his long-term recollections. Here again, the observable loss is not necessarily due to age per se, but could be related to the fact that society has destroyed the motivational force that governs memory.

Other factors which could effect memory are found almost exclusively in the stereotypic geronto. While occasionally the non-pathological aged person may appear to have lost this faculty, investigation would possibly show that even as a youth his memory was not good. With the geriatric or senescent individual, neuroses, psychoses, emotional changes, psychophysical readjustments with biological and somatic alterations may cause deterioration of memory. *The same conditions found in a younger individual could produce the same losses.*

Memory lapse in the later years is, then (irrespective of the theory of memory accepted by one), due primarily to changing perceptual abilities and to persistence of individual motivational forces. Other factors tend, generally, to be of pathological origin and not necessarily attributable to age alone. Until far more documented experimental data is available, the true nature of short-term and/or long-term memory loss must be largely a matter of conjecture.

Chapter Ten

ADJUSTMENT IN LATER LIFE

ADJUSTMENT is a term used by both psychologists and lay people. The latter group tends to use the term improperly. They consider that adjustment is indicated by desirable behavior. Actually, the term connotes either good and/or successful adjustment or maladjustment in terms of success or failure in meeting personal needs. Evaluation of the *goodness* or the *badness* of the behavior is not considered by the behavioral scientist.

Throughout life, the individual must constantly adjust environmental elements to meet current need or attune the self to the environment. If self and environment are compatible, the person is said to be adjusted; if not, he is considered maladjusted.

Any change, either of the environment or of the self, will require some level of readjustment. It is relatively easy to adjust to the physical background but problems frequently exist in the more difficult social and psychological areas which may be the more important. Basic to adequate adjustment at any age is a wholesome outlook and a realistic perception of life, emotional and social maturity, and a good balance between inner compulsions and social controls. Interpersonal relationships are most important since no one lives unto himself alone. As one goes about his daily activities, he must constantly interact with other individuals in a variety of situations. Adjustments must be made on a basis of relationships: with friends and enemies, employers and employees, with those of the same and opposite sex, young and old, rich and poor and with those who differ from ourselves in ways too numerous to consider here. The incompatible must be made compatible or *eliminated* if we hope to become truly adjusted.

The socially adequate person is one who can "get along" with people. Since his mores and attitudes are, as a rule, influenced by his culture, he recognizes his own problems and those of others in this specific milieu. When he has succeeded in adjusting in this environment, he will, in all probability, be able to modify adequately to compensate for normal change. If, however, he moves to a different cultural society, he will immediately face significant problems of adjustment in his interpersonal relations due to conflicting mores. Cultural reconditioning may prove a difficult task. Success in adjusting to his new environment will probably depend on the level of commitment to the old. The longer one has been committed to his convictions, the more difficult it will be to effect any significant adjustment to the new.

There are many stages in social development: infant and early childhood, preadolescent, adolescent, preadult, early maturity, later maturity and, finally, gerontological. Each stage provides certain specific problems and the older one becomes, the more he will be convinced that his convictions are uniquely proper.

During his lifetime, an individual is a member of many different groups. He assumes a distinctive role in each and usually accepts his relationships with others in terms of his position. If he cannot or will not accept his earned or assigned place in the hierarchy, he must effect a change in the social environment or in self. Failure in both of these efforts will lead to maladjustments at a level commensurate with the force of individual need and/or frustration and anxiety.

Frustration and anxiety frequently lead to aggressive behavior which, almost invariably, interferes with adjustment. It will, among other things, produce non–goal-directed behavior and frequently belligerence. Stress, tension and disruption of equilibrium may produce neuroses or psychoses which lead to conflict. This friction between external pressure and internal conviction frequently leads to conflict between judgment and expectations. The individual may then be faced with a variety of incompatible choices.

While social adjustment is probably of prime importance, there are many other significant areas we must consider. Among these we find emotional, personality, family life, occupational and leisure time. Each exists independently, but all are interrelated into the social to provide total personal adjustment or maladjustment. Probably no one can be considered as wholly adjusted nor, for that matter, totally maladjusted. Should one adjust completely to one of the many subcultures (drug, hippie, ethnic, poverty or the newly created subculture of the aged), he will probably find himself maladjusted to total society. The individual may be personally well-adjusted, but, from the point of view of society, completely maladjusted! In many cases one must, then, choose between personal and social adjustment, a futile choice. The wise individual will probably attempt to adjust to his particular subculture (if any) through a frame of reference provided by total culture. The result will probably be incomplete but *acceptable* adjustment to both the culture and the subculture.

It is a generally accepted fact that the old tend to be maladjusted. If this is true to any indicative degree, it is true *only* to those who are not themselves aged. While many gerontos are inadequately adjusted, it is doubtful if the percentage is significantly higher than may be found in any other age group.

The geronto *should* be better adjusted than a younger person because of greater capacity for adjustment. He should have developed a higher tolerance for frustration, a superior ability to cope and a considerably greater level of self-understanding and knowledge of human behavior, all of which should serve to increase his potential.

On the other hand, inability to accept a changed role in society, to understand his new reality, and failure to accomplish some of the developmental tasks of the gerontological period will inhibit adjustment in old age.

Human beings tend to take pride in the fact that their behavior —contrasted with that of lesser animals—represents the use of intellectual controls. All too often, however, the animal rather than the human qualities in man gain ascendency and emotional urges and compulsions replace objective reasoning and judgment. While human emotions are, as a rule, more sophisticated than those of other animals, they may be equally important in determining behavioral patterns.

Emotional expression results from the fusion of complex sensory experiences with patterns of behavior determined by society. A perceptual stimulus starts the emotional reaction which is experienced only when the feelings and other affective elements have been aroused through the functioning of the autonomic nervous system. With the assistance of the endocrine system, responses are diffused and spread throughout the organism. Emotions have both inherited and learned reaction patterns involving visceral behavior and affective experiences through the operation of the vital functions (change of heart action, respiration, and the release of hormones into the bloodstream) which energize the individual. All emotions seem to have at least three phases: the physiological changes (blood pressure, respiration, GSR, etc.), the emotional behavior (evidenced by such activities as laughing or crying) and the personal emotional experience or the *knowing* and *feeling*.

A specific stimulus is required to activate inherent potential and learned patterns into complex emotional experiences. Certain stimuli are emotion-arousing at one time although not at another, and to one individual while not to others. To be emotion-producing the stimulus must be related to goal-directed behavior.

The duration of an emotional response is determined by the persistence of the stimuli which may be real or vicarious. Training and experience are other factors that influence the effectiveness of an emotion-arousing stimulus. As the individual develops and matures, his needs, understandings, associations and changing goals and ambitions influence his emotional behavior. His health, both physical and mental, are critical elements in determining emotional reactions. The ill are easily aroused by stimuli that would not effect them were they well.

Emotional growth is a product of maturation and acculturation. Maturation is not necessarily a matter of age. A given youngster of fifteen may be far more mature than a particular individual of sixty. Just so, the young may be considerably more stable, emotionally, than the old. It is purely an individual matter. By the same token, there is no true relationship between age and social or cultural effectiveness. Changes in one's emotional stability, then, from youth until old age are determined in part by the relative *total* maturity of the individual at various ages. As a rule there will be only *slight* changes in emotional expression unless other important factors change.

It has often been suggested that the geronto tends to be emotionally unstable. With selected individuals this is, of course, true. These persons were probably unstable even in their younger years and should not be considered as typical of the age group. When true observable change does exist, the *cause* should be determined, and not merely assumed to be simply due to aging.

Old age per se does not produce emotional instability. Since emotional conditioning is complicated by inner conflict and previous emotional experience, physiological change and attitudes associated with self-interest may give positive direction to behavior. Changing attitudes may be important factors in observed emotional instability. These, combined with the frequent feeling of loss of personal maturity, may be important facets of the retirement syndrome. When this is true, the person may become highly emotional, not as a result of aging but, rather, because of a variety of associative factors. Thus, emotional adjustment, when necessary, may be effected only through stabilization of the many components and recognition of the retirement syndrome with its real and imagined influences on the older person and his abilities to compromise.

As we attempt to assess the possible changes in personality adjustment, we must accept, at least tentatively, a definition of this elusive quality. A categorical description is almost impossible despite the fact that there are many inherent characteristics including appearance, speech, aptitudes, skills, habits, knowledge, size, build, emotional reactions, attitudes, gait, and so forth. Some are innate, others result from learning and experience. Some are subject to continual modification, others are immutable.

The writer has accepted as his definition: "Personality is the sum total of the impact one individual has on others." It is a true gestalt. Since no two individuals possess the same hierarchy of traits, components, aspects or characteristics, no two people will have *identical* personalities. In the formative years, an individual will frequently attempt to develop a personality similar to that of one he may wish to emulate. While he cannot be completely successful, his total self may become quite comparable to his model.

Personality development is a continuing function, a neverending series of modifications. As the individual components change, knowledge increases, attitudes alter, emotions mature, self-concept stabilizes; thus the gestalt personality is modified and the social impact of the individual is determined.

Attempts have been made over the years to develop firm classifications of personality types. Hippocrates, about 400 B.C., suggested classification in terms of "body humors." The sanguine personality was quick, gay and unstable; the choleric, easily angered; the melancholic, pessimistic; and the phlegmatic, slow and unexitable. Sheldon, Stevens and Tucker classified personality types in terms of body build (endomorphic, mesomorphic or ectomorphic), while Spranger suggested classification in terms of postures toward other people. He considered the theoretical type as being metaphysical and scientific; the economic, as very business like; the aesthetic, as sensuous and unreliable; the social as interested in their fellows and in social movement; the political as power-seekers; and the religious as mystic, pietistic or missionary types. Another classification accepted by many is by endocrine character. The parathyroid is seen as explosive and aggressive; the hyperthyroid, as overambitious and domineering; the hypothyroid, as lazy and intellectually dull; the pituitary, as good-humored, patient, docile and tolerant; the hypergonadal, as aggressive; and the hypogonadal, as having a cultural bent. Jung classified personalities as introvert and extrovert and Freud as anal-erotic, oral-erotic and genital types. Each of these attempts to categorize personality is possibly defensible but certainly open to specific criticism.

It seems to the writer that a completely eclectic approach is more defensible than any categorizing attempt could possibly be. A combination of endocrine and social factors will greatly modify extroversion, introversion or ambiversion together with the somatotype to create a unique, individualized personality similar to many but identical to none. Each element found in the individual personality will continually change and modify until complete maturity has been achieved. During the mature years, modifications will be minimal unless the physical or mental condition changes through illness, accident or association. In the gerontological years, personality change will be in direct ratio to the type and rate of debilitation. Changing appearance, speech, habits, attitudes and emotional reactions together with alterations in the endocrine balance and social acceptance determine alterations in the gestalt personality. While modification is probably unavoidable as one ages, the well-integrated, highly effective personality will resist extreme change and tend to remain viable until almost complete debilitation takes place.

Adjustment to personality modification is rarely difficult but adjustment to major change is frequently traumatic. This is, however, a problem found only, as a usual rule, with the pathological segment of the aged. When the change is a concomitant of psychotic or neurotic conditions, psychiatric help will usually be required. This condition is rarely observed in the nonpathological majority of the gerontos where necessary adjustments present few real problems.

One of the most difficult areas of adjustment comes in the field of family life change. This problem was considered as a developmental task in Chapter Two, and as an area of potential weakness in Chapter Four. The older person will usually resist any shift in the family structure and may even refuse to adjust when change has transpired. Since the home is the first and probably the most significant agent in the adjustment of any individual towards successful living, refusal to accept unavoidable change here may lead to serious maladjustment.

From birth to maturity, continual change is not only acceptable, but most welcome, since each alteration tends to improve one's position. After maturity, many slight modifications will be observed, but none that produce maladjustment except in pathological cases. These changes are due, in major part, to new maturity of other family members and not to alterations of self.

As young adults, continuous change in the family is expected as a normal part of development. The husband-wife courtship and preparenthood relationship soon becomes routine and satisfying to the couple unless outside factors (parents, friends, associates) interfere. Every effort must be exerted by the couple to screen out external influences. With the birth of the first child, the intrusion of a third member calls for many adjustments. The mother must be sure that the father does not become a semi-isolate because of her preoccupation with the baby. By the same token, the father should not appear to be more interested and concerned with the new arrival than with the wife. As a usual rule, the required fine balance is achieved after a brief period of readjustment and a new level of maturity is attained. Inability to make these basic adjustments will probably indicate a definite immaturity that may be of neurotic or psychotic origin.

Each new arrival into the family circle serves to make new adjustment more necessary and more involved. Regardless of family size, the parents normally serve as decision-makers and leaders of the group. Some families are patriarchal, some matriarchal. More often today, however, we find an oligarchy with power resting in both parents and, on occasion, an older child.

As the children mature, the parent role changes. He becomes primarily an advisor, counselor and advocate and shares decision-making. Gradually, the relationship becomes almost totally reciprocal with the final decisions made jointly but with age being considered as an important weighing factor. The parent is a close friend, a confidant and, at times, banker to the almost independent adult children.

When the parent reaches the longevous period, a reversal of roles may frequently be observed. The children usurp parental prerogatives, one after another. Eventually, the roles become substantially reversed with the decision-making function passing from parent to child. This is a most difficult adjustment for the old person to make. Despite the fact that change begins as modification, it tends to accelerate to a point where trauma may be produced. The geronto loses his self-concept and becomes truly old. The children can prevent this situation from developing if they will be completely considerate at all times and if they will permit the parent to believe that their decisions were suggested by him. Adjustment to changing family life must come from outside; they can rarely be made by the old themselves.

In the longevous years, occupational adjustment becomes most important. The major reconciliation will, of course, be to retirement with the accompanying loss of employment or the change to less acceptable occupational activities. With most individuals, the entire productive life has been in either an area of high interest or one where personal ability to function adequately has made a satisfactory level of success possible.

While all too few are truly happy with their occupational life, most have effected compromise between ambition and opportunity and ability. Once this compromise has been reached, the individual tends to avoid change, *even to a preferred position,* since his security might be threatened. Throughout life, then, occupational compromise is the rule rather than the exception and adjustment to the status quo is essential to a satisfying life.

After a period of some thirty or forty years in the same, or a closely allied occupation, *a way of life* becomes established. The adjustments, where necessary, have been made and life becomes comfortable even though it may not be exciting. Of course, cultural change, job descriptions, changing individual potential and a multitude of other factors require continuous minor adjustments to one's occupation. This is modification, however, not change and as a rule creates no significant problems.

When the geronto faces mandatory retirement, one of the most difficult of all adjustments must be made. A way of life for many years is changed almost overnight and the individual reaches what seems to be a "dead end." He moves from a scheduled to an unscheduled day and life loses purpose. When the future is all in the past, life may cease to be worth living. This loss of purpose more often than not leads to an early death.

Adjustment to unemployment must be started *long before* the end of the years of occupation. A realization of the inevitability of retirement must be accepted and plans made for the jobless future. Hobbies and avocational activities must be developed to help fill the long days and, when possible, a second occupation in an uncrowded field should be considered. When ten or even twenty years are used to adjust to the problems of old age, the future will not seem so hopeless.

The individual whose retirement has been voluntary more frequently enjoys the lack of occupational responsibilities. He has probably been looking towards his new freedom with pleasure. While he may have a few problems in adjusting to change, he will shortly accept his new way of life and probably enjoy every minute of each day. This is especially true of that individual who has spent his life working at a job he hated.

The creative, imaginative person whose life has seen many

voluntary occupational changes, who has continually searched for a new challenge, who has been successful in a variety of activities, will look to retirement as "just another challenge!" His adjustment will be a very minor problem and he will continue to enjoy life to the fullest and to remain, until death, active and productive.

Occupational adjustment is, then, an individualized problem difficult for many, insignificant to a few. It must be faced throughout life and, prior to retirement, considered in great detail. Pre-retirement seminars and workshops should be provided for *all* over fifty years of age to prepare them for happy retirement and a productive old age.

The most difficult adjustment an old person must make is to the death of the spouse. In a continuing marriage relationship, a high level of interdependence is developed, and when that "other part of one" is gone, dependence must shift back to self or to others. If the partner that remains behind is truly mature, he will usually accept the responsibilities himself; if not, he will need to 'lean on" someone else. It is doubtful that anyone who has not experienced this tragedy can understand the degree of trauma produced nor the problems of adjustment that must be faced.

It has often been suggested that, after the loss of a loved one, a complete change of life including moving from the family home is beneficial. A new life in a new environment may be indicated for a few persons, but for the average individual, problems are multiplied. When life is continued in the same home, only one major adjustment needs to be effected—to the loss of the spouse. When a move is made to a new location, many compromises are required—a new home, new friends, new acquaintances, new stores, new and different problems require countless adjustments; some simple, others difficult. In a new environment, the sources of strength and support found in the old are missing. The geronto must stand alone. While it could be true that the countless new problems may tend to reduce preoccupation with the loss of the spouse, they merely extend the time necessary to make the prime adjustment. One major adjustment, regardless of its severity, is easier to make than a dozen less arduous compromises.

Adjustment must, in this difficult sphere, be made in terms of happy memories, vicarious substitutions, new involvements and, possibly, a fresh dedication to service. Many times the only adequate solution lies in remarriage. This step will be successful *only* if the children and other interested relatives and friends give at least tacit support. They must realize that the new spouse does not supplant even the memory of the old, but does provide a brand-new, completely separate reason for living.

Life, from beginning to end, is a never-ceasing series of adjustments and compromises. Unless these are accomplished to a satisfactory degree, an individual cannot adequately relate to society. Areas of adjustment suggested in the preceeding are not necessarily unique to the aged, but are probably more important in the later years. Other adjustments made in the preadult periods, together with the modifications achieved during the mature years, will not, as a usual rule, become severe problems to the old.

One must remember that each human being is exceptional and, as a result, no two will find need for adjustment in the same areas. A problem to one is a simple function to another. When one appears maladjusted then, we must search for the particular problem areas if we hope to gain those insights necessary to understanding.

Chapter Eleven

THE PERSONALITY OF THE GERONTO

THE personality of the geronto is undoubtedly different from that he exhibited as a mature man in middle life. No moreso, in all probability, than the differences evidenced between the preadult period and the middle years. In both cases the disparity could (and probably should) be considered not so much personality *change* as *modification*. Change would indicate complete replacement of personality components, but modification is usually accomplished solely by alteration of existing elements.

Definitions of personality vary greatly among psychologists. Merely as a point of departure, the writer suggests the following: "Personality is the total impact one individual may have on others." It is the product of many elements integrated into a gestalt totality. Among the elements are personal appearances, physical size, color, voice quality, diction, concepts, prejudices, understandings, talents, abilities, level of compassion and a variety of imponderables which remain unidentified. Since the above is true, no two people have identical personalities but similar composites frequently exist. One tends to respond favorably to others with personality elements very like his own or to those having a totality he himself should like to possess.

THE NORMAL PERSONALITY

The roots of personality must certainly lie in childhood. Among long-accepted theories we find the psychoanalytic and the genetic-developmental. Freud and his followers believe that each of us is a different person because of the distinctive pattern of relationships which develop between the id, ego and superego. Normal development requires the emergence of an adequate ego (that controlling force emerging through socialization and representing the conscious aspects of mental life) which is capable of regulating the release of id energies (those inherited masses of energy which are considered by Freudian disciples to be the repository of our sex and mastery drives, hedonistic forces, and aggressive tendencies). The superego, consisting of the conscience and the ego ideal, must be in complete control of the id and the ego to provide a set of inner moral principles to guide individual conduct.

Many students of human behavior consider the psychoanalytical interpretation of personality to be too nebulous and almost totally animalistic. They consider genetic roots of personality to be found in the developmental process of growth, learning, and maturation which is guided by the total growth experience and not by any hierarchy of factors or forces which may be easily categorized.

The writer tends to accept the genetic-developmental theory—with certain modifications—as a base on which individual personality may develop. Changes in self-concept, in environment and in need, together with innumerable physical alterations, continually modify the basic personality and tend to make it more unique and individualistic.

The importance of early experience on later behavior is probably greatly exaggerated by the influence of animal studies which consistently show such effects. Studies of human beings *do not* indicate as strong a primacy effect of early experience as was once believed. This suggests that in order to understand behavior we must place far more emphasis upon analysis of the person's contemporary social situation and the continually changing environment which plays such a major role in personality development.

During childhood, preadolescence, adolescence and early maturity, there is continuing modification of individual personality. This is due to physical changes, reflection of personality attributes observed in others that impress the individual, experienced success or failure in personal effectiveness, changing self-concept and a multitude of other possibly unique factors. These are all a part of maturational development. When maturity is achieved, the personality will be rather complete—effective or ineffective, adequate or inadequate, pleasant or unpleasant, as the case may be. From this time on throughout life, continuous modification may or may not be observed. Changes rarely occur except through long periods of modification. If the personality achieves desired ends and satisfies the individual, little modification will take place except through interaction with a changing environment.

One important factor in human development is frequently overlooked. This is the matter of personality utilization. Here individual motivation may be the determining factor. The highly motivated individual will tend to exert the force of his personality on others while the person with lesser motivation will permit his personality potential to remain dormant. As motivation varies, personality expression tends to shift. Other psychological (and physiological) changes and modifications which take place during aging may produce certain personality modifications, e.g. perceptual loss, biological deterioration, together with various somatic and emotional modifications may possibly alter the total personality.

True *change* in personality may be found in certain older people. Where the geronto is geriatric (ill) or senescent (losing his mental faculties), personality may be drastically altered. Many severe neurotic and almost all psychotic reactions lead to such alterations. Since the pathological segment of the gerontological population comprises only a scant 10 per cent of the total group, the importance of personality shift is not great and is probably only slightly more notable than in other age segments. In younger groups, the true reasons for unusual change (illness and/or mental deterioration) are recognized; in the geronto, age itself is considered the sole reason. Since the stereotype of the "old man" is drawn from the pathological 10 per cent, it is almost universally accepted that personality deterioration is an inevitable concomitant of aging. This is another of the many myths resulting from inappropriate categorization.

Personality modification which does take place in aging may be slight or of considerable consequence. It will depend almost entirely on psychological change or modification in the several basic areas. Readjustment is a task of aging. The normal (nonpathological) geronto remains relatively well-adjusted and realistic in his appraisal of facts. The superior individual (intellectually, physically, emotionally, etc.) will usually tend to retain his basic personality organization better than do other segments of the population. Many times the older person's personality is more consistent than are those of younger people since he may be bothered less by anxiety. In addition, the superior individual can see the many *advantages* of the older years and become much more effective in mastering the developmental tasks of the period. He retains much of his capacity for original thinking together with a high-level ingenuity in solving practical problems. He may, however, tend to become obsessive, restless and intolerant of the weaknesses of others—young or old! Attitudes may become more rigid and prejudices more dominant.

Married individuals normally remain better adjusted. They are infrequently defensive and their emotional relationships with others continue to be warm and their cultural interests strong. They have fewer neurotic symptoms than single persons and maintain a higher level of interest in life and living. They seem, as a rule, to have more idealistic purposes. The single person, while not as well-adjusted nor as adaptable as the married, will retain a high level of his potential as long as he remains nonpathological.

Physical changes produce the more significant shifts in personality. As the bearing changes, the appearance loses its vitality, the voice its resonance, and more noticeable modifications of personality. These tend to be gradual and true individual effectiveness is not as greatly minimized as one might expect.

We need to develop more completely the concept that the geronto has not a "different" but merely a "modified" personality as long as he remains nonpathological. With proper guidance almost all of the older population can remain effective throughout their later years and retain their expanded personality along with personal independence until the end.

PERSONALITY DEVIATIONS

In far too many instances, the personality of the older individual is evaluated as having recently changed when it may have *long been maladjusted.* Only through continual observations of a person from early maturity can it be determined if a maladjustment is truly a result of aging or if it should be considered to be an abnormality that developed long before the gerontological period was reached.

There are many types of personality deviations found in individuals who are neither neurotic or psychotic. There are the "peculiar," the "weird," the "unusual," the "funny" people found in every age group in every society. Their behavior, while departing from the norm, is not so extreme as to indicate need for extensive treatment or separation from the social group. It is not usually possible to fit these people into definite categories of disorder purely on a basis of the behavior they exhibit. Symptoms are, indeed, quite deceiving, for two people with the same problem may display very different manifestations, while two others with different problems may exhibit similar symptoms. We may be able to group a collection of symptoms into a pattern called a syndrome, give the syndrome a name and consider it as a fairly definite entity. We will use the term personality deviation to refer to those in our society who are not maladjusted in either a clinical or legal sense but who have developed behavioral patterns which are not socially acceptable or personally adequate. While it may be true that these syndromes *can* develop in the older years, a great majority of the deviations have long been present even though they may have been sublimated.

While there is no precise way to classify these personality disorders, we will attempt to label a few deviations which are frequently observed. Every community has its *eccentric character:* The little old lady who wears a heavy coat in the summertime and saves string, bottles and old paper; the young man who prefers to lie rather than to tell the truth; the person who talks to himself or to a variety of inanimate objects; the rugged individualist so divorced from reality that he lives outside the mainstream of society. There are also men who prefer to dress like women and women who dress like men as well as parasitic and "remittance" men and women who live off their families and friends and refuse to contribute to their welfare or comfort in any way. These people, and many like them in somewhat different ways, may know and not care, or may fail to realize that they are different. While not sufficiently detached from reality to be classed as neurotic or psychotic, any increase in the intensity of the syndrome could lead to serious maladjustment. These are the eccentrics!

The *social isolates* and *social rejects* form another class of deviates. The isolate withdraws from society of his own volition for any number of purely personal reasons. He may feel inferior to the group or so superior that the average person bores him. Either feeling, if not sublimated, may prevent social assimilation. The individual with feelings of inferiority will frequently cross the street to avoid meeting an acquaintance and may tend to prefer the life of a recluse. If he remains in the social stream, he may become a whining, self-deprecating nervous bore. As compensation, certain of these individuals adopt airs of aggressiveness and become autocratic and overbearing, behavior which is probably even more objectionable to other people. Those with feelings of superiority, on the other hand, rarely enter any social situation as a matter of choice.

The social reject is frequently anxious to be a part of the mainstream of life but, for any of a variety of reasons, is rejected by his peers. Reasons range from repulsive appearance to objectionable personal habits. Almost invariably the social reject becomes a recluse or a "loner" but not, as a rule, from personal choice.

The *dependent* individual belongs to another less-than-normal segment of the population. He may have failed as a child to master the developmental task of achieving the adequate balance between dependence-independence which is so necessary in our society. He may be passive, indecisive, lack initiative and lean on others for support, guidance and protection. He is among the most pathetic of maladjusted persons. When he cannot make decisions and is unable to stand up for his own rights, when normal situations are to him formidable obstacles, he must always be protected by others. As long as he is shielded, he may be happy and content, but can rarely adjust to interdependent living.

There are also many transient personality disorders which may occur in any individual who is exposed to undue stress or anxiety. He may break in any number of ways and will probably verbalize his feelings by such remarks as "I just can't take it anymore," or "I am sick of living in this rat race," or "I am just tired."

The personality deviations described above are only a few of the many that may be observed in almost any community. You will probably recognize these stereotypes among your friends and acquaintances. They are all reflections of some deviation in a person's mental and emotional orientation and can be observed in every age group from childhood through old age. Paranoid delusions, obsessions, disorders of consciousness, memory lapses, mental aberrations and sexual deviations are other problems often observed. All may develop into definite neuroses or psychoses, for it is merely a matter of degree.

While every deviation we have mentioned may be observed in the gerontological population, *none is unique to this group.* The same deviations may be found among children, preadolescents, adolescents, and at every age among the adult population— and in equal, if not greater, numbers. Since there is always the tendency to evaluate the old in terms of the pathological 10 per cent, the man on the street will believe that personality deviations are to be expected in the older population.

Every effort must be made to educate the public to understand that while the personality of the geronto may become modified, it will not, except in pathological cases, disintegrate or deviate to any significant extent merely because of aging.

Personality will usually remain within normal ranges and effective until death.

THE ABNORMAL PERSONALITY

There are many types of personality abnormalities. Some are quite serious, others merely incapacitating. It is frequently suggested that the percentage of maladjusted individuals is far greater in the gerontological population than in any younger group. While this may actually be true, the writer is inclined to reject this premise. We probably discover more neurotics and psychotics in the older population simply because we anticipate that they will exhibit aberrant behavior and observe them more closely. It seems doubtful that the geronto will become newly abnormal unless he has possessed latent tendencies since childhood or at least since young adulthood.

Senescence is not an abnormality in the true sense of the word. It is *inevitable* if one lives long enough! Thank God a majority die before they reach this final stage in development. The age at which one reaches senility varies greatly from person to person. One may, in today's society, expect to remain intellectually functional until perhaps age ninety or even one hundred.

The material presented in this chapter is projected from the frame of reference suggested above.

The Neurotic

The neurotic fears things inside himself. Any thought, feeling or urge whose expression is subject to punishment may produce a neurosis. This is especially true when the individual takes steps to hide but not to abolish the compulsion. As a consequence, undesirable social behavior and an increase in self-debilitation may result when anxiety becomes intolerable.

Anxiety builds up within the person if repression or sublimation fails to provide the necessary catharsis. Many times an individual who has been able to control his neuroses throughout most of his life will, in old age, find the situation has become intolerable. When this happens, he may display obsessive and/or compulsive reactions. Sexual fantasies are common as are other types of satisfying vicarious experience.

In many cases the neurosis may be focused on one object or situation and will then be considered a phobia. These are almost always harmless and are reflected in dress, performance and the studious rejection and/or fear of objects, people or situations.

In very rare cases, an urge to murder or inflict physical injury on another may result from severe neuroses. These are, however, rarely problems with the neurotic geronto and are probably more frequently observed in a younger population.

Where a collection of physical symptoms accompanies neuroses, hysteria will frequently develop. The hysteric may become incapacitated by a variety of problems of psychosomatic origin. Blindness, loss of speech, loss of the sense of touch, an assortment of severe, nonorganic pains or catatonia may result. These have been observed in every age group and should not be considered as unique to the gerontological population. They may appear at any time and are rooted in neuroses of either long or short duration. It is possible that they may be more severe and more significant in an older person than in a more resilient younger individual. The geronto is frequently labeled senescent and as such is more apt to be committed to an institution.

When a neurotic fails to solve his life problems and is unable to cope with normal conflicts or manage his interpersonal relations, the outcome may be such complete depression that the individual becomes apathetic and ceases to function adequately. When completely depressed, the person may withdraw socially, become lethargic, hopeless and helpless and may even find that mental and intellectual functioning is severely impaired.

The loss of a loved one, of a position, or any other severe personal decrement may induce reactive depression. The major difference between reactive depression and the usual mood change to which all humans are subject lies in the duration and intensity. Many neurotics seem somewhat depressed throughout their lives and their depression deepens significantly in times of crisis. The geronto is frequently faced with personal loss of such magnitude that he may become a victim of reactive depression. The prime problem is, of course, the loss of the spouse. Many times the bereaved person fails to recover from his depression and his entire future is placed in jeopardy. The second major cause of reactive depression in the older person is mandatory retirement. This event is all to frequently considered the "beginning of the end." Despite the fact that this is *not true*, it has become an accepted concept and the idea is often fostered by the many agencies designed to "serve" the old and to remove them from the mainstream of life and from competition with the young by providing opportunities for noninvolvement.

Even though depression is noted with some frequency among the aged, it is not unique to this population segment. The final break may come in the older years but the neurotic roots are almost always found in a younger period.

The Psychotic

The major difference between a neurotic and a psychotic must lie in the fact that while the former may build castles in the air, the latter lives in them. Of course, the psychiatrist collects the rent!

While the neurotic is handicapped rather severely in interpersonal relationships and by emotional instability, and while his life is confused by a variety of unresolved problems and distorted perceptions, he usually continues to exist within the limits of social expectation. Psychoses have the same base in tension, anxiety and continuing threats to self. If the psychotic does not have the human resources necessary to cope with his problems, he, unlike the neurotic, gives up and withdraws from life altogether.

Since psychosis is not a single disease, it has no single cause or uniform treatment. When any hierarchy of symptoms indicates that the ego or self may be in serious conflict with life, the diagnosis is usually psychosis. Many attempts have been made to determine the underlying causes of various psychoses. Either inherited genetic composites or biochemical imbalance may account for the disorder. Neither of these postulates has, however, been proven beyond scientific doubt. More frequently the theorist attributes these most serious disorders to childhood experience where the individual overreacted to stress and failure to cope satisfactorily. In order to live with his problems, he adopted abnormal perceptions, actions, and methods of thinking, and indefensible motivations. Thus, the psychotic learns to respond in ways that deviate considerably from accepted norms.

Any attempt to classify human disorders must be a complicated procedure. Diagnosticians rarely agree about the label to fit to any individual patient. If we contend that various psychotics should be more alike than different, we are in error. The writer hesitates to refer to the psychotic as being "ill" and doubts that the term "mental illness" can be used within any medical framework. The term "personality deformity" should possibly replace "mental illness." Over the years, however, a variety of terms have been accepted as labels for behavioral abnormalities.

We will consider a few of those more frequently observed and attempt to determine if any may be considered particular problems to the aged.

Simple Schizophrenia

Any individual who is abnormally apathetic, seclusive, rejective of social contact, dull, and unresponsive, and who finds any uncomplicated life style to be preferable is usually labeled a *simple schizophrenic*. Tramps, prostitutes, pickpockets and petty thieves frequently come from this population segment. They are rarely subject to hallucinations or delusions nor do they act in bizarre ways. They merely reduce contacts with others to a bare minimum and may engage in orgies of "self-pity." All tend to exist but never to really live.

Hebephrenic Schizophrenia

The popular stereotype of the schizophrenic is based on the bizarre behavior of those suffering from severe personality disintegration. These are the *hebephrenic schizophrenics* whose speech tends to be incoherent and unintelligible, who may laugh or giggle at inappropriate times and who live in private worlds of fantasy and delusion. One may believe himself to be Jesus Christ, Napoleon or the embodiment of evil. He may even believe that the end of the world has come and that he is the sole survivor. At times, this person may either lose control of bladder and bowels or may *just not care to control their functioning*. He departs totally from the real world and lives, usually not too contentedly, in a private personal world.

Catatonic Schizophrenia

The *catatonic schizophrenic* frequently holds himself in a painful and rigid posture for hours and shows no response to the physical discomfort. He does not respond to sound or sight, nor to pressure or pain. While oblivious to all outside stimulation, he is usually preoccupied with hallucinations of whispered voices that threaten, together with horrible sounds and visions. This is a very dramatic, emergency attempt to cope with overwhelming problems he cannot escape.

Paranoid Schizophrenia

The *paranoid schizophrenic's* difficulty tends to lie in his complete lack of trust in others. He feels that he must continually watch people since they are all plotting against him because of their intense jealousy of his great knowledge and superior abilities. These grandiose paranoid delusions of persecution may make this type of schizophrenic truly dangerous. He may retaliate against his "enemies" merely in considered self-protection.

Among the gerontological population, each type of schizophrenia may be observed. There are probably more simple schizophrenics and fewer catatonics with an almost average number of hebephrenics and paranoiacs. Whenever abnormalities are discovered, even though apparently of new origin, the roots will almost always be traceable to childhood. With aging, the individual may lose the effectiveness of his defenses. The senescent or geriatric individual will far more frequently develop schizophrenia than will the members of the more normal gerontological population.

At least 10 per cent and possibly as many as 15 per cent of those committed to institutions each year are diagnosed as suffering from emotional or affective reactions. Emotional maladjustments may be intensified by disorders of the schizophrenic process or its disintegration. Some 75 per cent of this category are female.

Mania

About one-third of the group displaying symptoms of agitation, excitement, failing judgment and deterioration of interpersonal relations are classed as *manic*. As this condition intensifies, all activity (including speech) speeds up and any interference annoys the individual. In the final stages, the manic becomes close to delirium and is confused, incoherent and disoriented. He may need to be physically restrained to prevent danger to himself or to others.

Depression

Another one-third are diagnosed as *depressive*. Here again we have an exaggeration of the moods all persons experience in some degree. As with many abnormalities, it is merely a matter of degree. When the deepening depression becomes disorienting, the individual becomes preoccupied with a feeling of failure, worthlessness, sinfulness and deep despair. Some patients alternate between manic and depressive states. When in the latter, they tend to cut themselves off from society and may contemplate suicide. On occasion these persons may reach such stuporous levels that they become bedridden.

Agitation

The remaining one-third suffering from affective reactions are the *agitated*. They become quite depressed, but the level of agitation, activity and excitement accelerates. They become worried and harried and may indulge in orgies of self-pity. Fears of attacks from outside merely reflect the personal psychological condition.

Summary

There is no evidence presently available to indicate a more significant percentage of patients from these categories among the gerontological population. These severe personality disorders do not, as a rule, respond too favorably to treatment and prognosis is not good. Again, the determining factor must be degree. Many are able to function moderately in society if the condition remains at a low level.

Psychoses which result from acute and severe brain disorders will, it is feared, become increasingly common as preventative medicine, good nutrition and other factors extend the life span. While patients seventy years of age and older form as much as 30 per cent of admissions to mental hospitals, only where cerebral arteriosclerosis (hardening of the arteries) and certain other forms of senile brain damage exists can these be attributed to aging. Even in many of these cases, the condition is not of recent origin but only now is recognized because controls which the patient was once able to exert over his emotions, thoughts and behavior seem to deteriorate and become ineffectual. Thus, a condition which has existed since young adulthood in many cases, finally becomes obvious.

OTHER ABNORMALITIES

The Sociopathic Personality

There are many types of personality abnormalities classed as neither neuroses or psychoses. The *sociopath,* whose problem usually stems from his failure to develop a conscience, is irresponsible, self-centered, rebellious towards society and tends to prey on others as a way of life. He is egocentric, impulsive, irresponsible, cannot face failure and is always able to rationalize any behavior. This is an abnormality found less frequently in the aged population than among youth.

Sexual Deviance

The *sexual deviate* is the individual who fails to accept whatever standards of proper behavior are currently espoused by society. One who might have been considered a deviate fifty years ago could possibly be quite normal by today's standards. Each person must have a biological sexual identity. In addition, he must discover and accept his psycho-socio-biological sex role. If he cannot accept his biological self psychologically and demonstrate his social acceptance of both, he may possibly become a deviate. Among the forms such deviations take are homosexual behavior, pedophilia, beastiality, incest, fetishism, masturbation, exhibitionism, voyeurism, transvestism and sadism or masochism. Among the elderly, masturbation, exhibitionism and pedophilia (relations with children) are observed most frequently. In many cases, activities that may be considered quite ordinary for a youth are considered deviations if practiced by a geronto. Masturbation, which is today considered as normal (it was once thought to make one's "brain soft!") for youngsters, is deviant behavior in the old—despite the fact that the same reasons for the practice are found in the two groups. Opportunities for more normal sexual release are not usually available to the youth nor to the old person without a spouse.

The elderly individual may approach children simply because he fears rejection by an older person and fails to consider the consequences if any disclosure of his action is made. Exhibitionism may provide a certain vicarious satisfaction and seems to the culprit to be completely harmless. It may be that a diminishing of sexual potency may be one factor causing certain types of deviant behavior as compensation. Whatever the causes, the increase in observed frequency between the old and a younger segment of the population is not too significant. In addition, many practices considered normal for the young are believed to be abnormal when practiced by the old.

TREATMENT OF ABNORMALITIES

Today there are many types of treatment available for use with the various personality abnormalities. Somatic therapy and psychosurgery are infrequently used today since the various tranquilizers and psychotherapy have proven to be more effective. A majority of even the most severe abnormalities can be controlled *(but not cured)* by use of tranquilizers. As a result, the population of mental hospitals is being reduced each year. In only one category, those under age sixteen, is there an increase. Among the gerontological population, only the senescent who require continual supervision and medication and the geriatric who need to be cared for by trained personnel are institutionalized.

In summation, personality abnormalities are found in *every* age group from early childhood until death. Certain types of deviations may appear slightly higher at various ages. In all probability, the percentage at any age level will be fairly constant. At older ages, however, persons lose the ability to compensate and may no longer be able to cope with their problems. As a result, certain abnormalities which have long been present are noticed by others for the first time. When this happens, the layman immediately confirms his suspicion that a majority of personality abnormalities are a product of the aging process.

Chapter Twelve

BIOLOGICAL AGING

THE true roots of biological aging have not been specifically determined. A number of interesting theories have been proposed, all with some basis in research and experimentation. A program of continuing research should be initiated to not only determine precise causes, but also to attempt to discover possible deterrents.

One interesting theory is based on discoveries regarding the chemistry and mechanics of heredity. Crick, Watson and Wilkins, winners of the 1962 Nobel Prize for Medicine and Physiology, determined that chromosomes are made up of DNA whose atoms are arranged in long strands twisted together in a very complex double spiral. The genes, which are distinct segments of DNA having precise length and innate function, are the determinates of heredity. The order in which the atoms are found in a particular gene governs the genetic functioning of the individual. Potential tends to be passed on from generation to generation through transmitted chromosome structure and components. The genes, with material recorded on the strands, are theorized to program potential development and growth in all areas. While the functioning of genetic programming is most efficient, it has not been developed to cope indefinitely with the long-term consequences of illness, injury, infection and the non-renewal of nerve cells which may be rather severe. This long-term inadequacy of the genetic program may possibly mean that we do not grow old by design, but rather by inadequacies of nature and through human error.

Another theory which has gained certain acceptance is the theory of environmental aging. Animal experimentation has shown that the effects of ionizing radiation tend to be cumulative and to lead to early death of many exposed organisms from not one but a variety of causes. Adverse effects of radiation are greater for older animals, probably because older animals have weaker powers of resistance, recovery and restoration. Extremes of temperature, rarefied air, pollution and, possibly, an increase of stress conditions will shorten the life of any animal. While little or no experimental data are available concerning effects on human life, it may be assumed that man, as do all lesser animals, deteriorates from substantially the same causes. In addition, the cumulative effect of "accidents" which affect the hundreds of millions of cells which compose the human body and the accelerated disintegration of these cells with an accompanying deceleration of replacement leads to continuing biological aging.

Many of man's biological functions are rhythmic and/or periodic. The heartbeat, respiration, ovulation, certain electrical impulses in the brain and synaptic transmission reflect an almost "clock-like" precision in physiological functioning. Any interruption or even alteration of rhythms or periodicy may produce aging. Much experimentation is necessary to determine the time effects of these shifts. Why are rhythms interrupted? Are these changes results of or causes of aging? Increased understanding of biological rhythms could lead to increased longevity.

The importance of hormonal balance must never be minimized. The various endocrine (ductless) glands secrete their chemical substances directly into the bloodstream. These glands can be tentatively classified into three groups: those regulating specific aspects of metabolism (e.g. the islands of Langerhans which secrete insulin), those that function in conjunction with the autonomic nervous system (e.g. the adrenal medulla) and those which seem to have more permanent effects on the development and integration of the body, (e.g. the thyroid, gonads, adrenal cortex and pituitary). The *thyroid* stimulates metabolism and serves as a catalyst in the oxidation process regulating energy consumption. The *adrenals* secrete adrenaline together with a variety of chemicals whose prime function is to regulate carbohydrate metabolism and salt balance in the body. The *gonads* produce reproductive cells and secrete those hormones responsible for both primary and secondary sexual development. The *pituitary* is often called "master gland" since it seems to regulate the activities of all others.

Replacement of the sex hormones (estrogen and testosterone) plays an important part not only in relieving symptoms, but in slowing down the aging process and in the prevention of degenerative diseases of old age. We do not know specifically how hormones act. The general concensus is that they serve as catalysts in the various biochemical processes. Hormone concentrations are small in relation to the amplitude of the metabolic responses which they trigger.

All of the endocrine glands have specific but interrelated functions. They atrophy, disintegrate and change rate of functioning at various ages. Thus, there tends to be a different endocrine balance for each person at each age. Just how important endocrine homeostasis may be to aging has not as yet been determined, nor has any consensus been reached concerning the question of cause or result. In all probability, changes in functioning of the endocrine glands can be charged to the inadequate replacement of disintegrating cells so frequently observed in all physiological areas.

All of the vital organs in the body appear to eventually disintegrate or become less functional. There is, however, no specific sequence or rate observable in any two different individuals. With one person accelerated decay may be observed in the heart; with another, the kidneys or liver. Whether this is a result of genetic weakness, of illness, personal abuse or merely an "accident" in development has not been determined. Muscles and nerve tissues, where mitosis (cell division by a spindle where identical chromosomes move to opposite poles of the spindle and divide into two identical portions) slows down, will gradually deteriorate. On the other hand, cells like those in the liver and pancreas, where cellular division continues at higher levels, age far more slowly. It has not, as yet, been specifically ascertained whether inadequate endocrine functioning may be one of the prime causes of organic decay. We need to know also whether environment—either general or specific—may be considered a causative factor in the aging of particular organs as it seems to be in a more general way.

The overall functioning of the body is determined, at least in part, by physiological homeostasis. This, of course, refers to maintained balance in that series of physiological mechanisms which regulate and stabilize the "internal environment." Only when an adequate blood sugar balance is maintained, a proper acid-base relationship assured and equity established among the electrolytes can the body truly function within acceptable limits.

Among "failures" in homeostasis we find diabetes (a severe change in blood sugar balance) and any significant increase of acid level in the normally slightly alkaline blood. Strenuous exercise produces a temporary increase of acid level. Good homeostasis must depend, then, on the rate of recovery. With the young person in relatively good physical condition, recovery is usually quite rapid. On the other hand, if the individual is not fit, recuperation slows down and the imbalance may prove significant. With aging, lesser amounts of exercise become effectively strenuous and the capacity for recovery tends to decline. Thus, problems present at any age become possibly more significant with the passing years.

Any change in the electrolyte balance must be considered indicative. Such change is probably evidence of a problem rather than the cause of one. A study of the electrolytes and the aging process might possibly be a productive effort for geriatricians. It might be discovered that electrolyte imbalance may be a *cause* rather than a *result* of aging.

Balanced function of the bodily organs is necessary to the maintenance of complete homeostasis. The different rates of deterioration in the various organs cannot be predicted nor controlled. Homeostatic mechanisms must be flexible enough to cope with unusual variations. They must, for example, adjust to variations in physical effort or changes in temperature and food intake; they must operate appropriately during sleep, following injury or infection and with changes in organic functioning. There is considerable evidence to indicate that either homeostasis is less efficient in older people or that problems become more significant.

A majority of physical functions such as heart rate, metabolic rate, respiration, blood pressure and kidney and liver functions have a range of values which permit an individual to adapt to different surroundings, activities and relative conditions. These tolerance liminals may be reduced as aging takes place or when stabilizing mechanisms are sluggish or physiological adaptability of the individual is reduced.

A general reduction of physiological efficiency must be expected as a natural concomitant of aging. While it is certainly true that the normal geronto will not disintegrate as rapidly or completely as one who is geriatric or senescent and that he may adequately function to possibly extreme age, nothing will halt the complex developmental changes that lead eventually to deterioration of the mature organism and ultimately to its death. Percentage of decline varies from organ to organ and from function to function. The average decline in a human male from age thirty to seventy-five will be as follows:

Characteristic	*Per cent Decline*
Weight of brain	44
Number of axons in spinal nerve	37
Velocity of nerve impulses	10
Number of taste buds	64
Blood supply to brain	20
Output of heart at rest	30
Speed of return to normal pH of blood after displacement	83
Number of glomeruli in kidney	44
Vital capacity of lungs	44
Maximum oxygen uptake during exercise	60

Despite all arguments to the contrary, aging is probably not biologically inevitable. "Natural death" *never* occurs among unicellular organisms. Many protozoans, where the individual and reproductive cells are one and the same, can survive indefinitely! Certain human tissue culture lines may be said to be immortal. If individual cells are possibly deathless, why then, are multicellular organisms vulnerable? Is it due to inevitable "wear and tear" or to accidental pathological change? Is the cellular environment responsible for the death of the cells or has the breeding of higher forms of life with many specialized functions weakened the individual cells?

The genetic material in the nucleus of a cell (DNA) contains a program of instruction which is transmitted in the form of a code to the dividing cell and which regulates the vital protein synthesis for growth, repair of tissues and reproduction. Errors in the DNA code transmission induced by changes in the sequence of its bases or by cross-linkage of molecules cause erroneous messages to be transmitted to the dividing cells. These errors in genetic transmission manifest themselves in structurally and functionally inferior cells, characteristic of *old* tissues. New cells may change their characteristics completely (mutation) with serious consequences. These new cells may either not function normally or die and be replaced by fibrous tissue which is one of the features of degeneration, or the mutated cells may become independent, not function normally and develop into malignant cells.

It is true, of course, that the more sophisticated an animal becomes the greater will be the number of highly distinctive cells found in its organic structure. Man, through breeding, has become so complex that a wide variety of completely specialized cells are required to implement his unique functions. Exceptional cells are far more dependent and more vulnerable than are undifferentiated cells. Nonspecialized varieties grow more speedily, divide at a more rapid rate and possess more vitality than do their specialized progeny. It may be possible that, as a result of aging, functioning may become less effective due to a decrease of specialized and an increase of nonspecialized cells throughout the body.

During the peak human years (physically, between 18 and 25), the organs and glands of the body may function at as much as 150 per cent of minimal need. During these times, homeostasis is rather easily maintained. There is a gradual but accelerating decrease in organic and glandular function until, during the gerontological years, less than the minimal requirements are produced. With continued but uneven deceleration, homeostasis becomes impossible and physiological impairment, noticeable. Aging could then be considered as, at least partially, due to the replacement of specialized with nonspecialized cells.

When we credit pathological change to aging, are we suggesting that age and only age produces climate for adverse change? Is hypertension—the usual diagnosis of those with abnormally high blood pressures—a disease or a product of aging? Is it a cause or a result? What should be the criteria for any diagnosis of hypertension? There are many older individuals who have no problems with hypertension, thus, it cannot be considered an inevitable result of aging. Is it, perhaps, then a cause?

Arteriosclerosis was once considered inevitable and irreversible with the aged. Today we recognize that environmental factors and diet are probably the true cause of this condition. It has been discovered that arteriosclerosis tends to be accelerated with patients suffering from diabetes, myxedema (a diseased condition of the skin, characterized by dryness and swelling due to thyroid deficiency) and nephritis. Thus, even in conditions once thought to be primary and due solely to aging, we are discovering a variety of contributing causes. Cholesterol buildup has been shown to result from faulty diet and a deficiency of the B-complex vitamins, especially choline bitartrate which is so necessary to adequate liver functioning. These are only two examples of conditions once believed to be *caused* by aging which have proven to be primarily related to other factors.

There are certain types of illness which tend to be observed more frequently in the gerontological population. By the same token certain other conditions are found more frequently among children, in an adolescent population, or the young adult group. In all probability, the hormonal balance and/or the relative functioning of bodily organs characteristic of the various age groups provides the proper climate for specific conditions. Biological *change* is continuous from conception until death. Why, then, do we tend to consider biological aging as unique? Why not merely consider it as another period in biological development? Are changes produced by aging or do they cause aging? If change can be inhibited, can life be prolonged? If it can be prolonged, should it be? Are not aging and death advantageous to the evolutionary progress of man? These are among the many questions that require answers if we wish to truly understand biological aging, its causes, effects and, most important of all, its purpose!

Chapter Thirteen
AGING AND DELINQUENCY

DELINQUENCY and criminality are sociolegal rather than psychological terms. The juvenile offender is normally considered delinquent; the adult, criminal. We must assume in advance of any study of deviant behavior that we will discover many varieties of personality types and many, many contributing causes. Delinquent and criminal behavior are determined primarily as deviations from social demeanor as prescribed by the mores and the laws.

Behavior may be called delinquent in one society when the same conduct would be viewed not only as acceptable but desirable in another culture. Conformity to the standards of any subculture may be considered criminal by the major society. By the same token, behavior which is tolerated when discovered in one age group will be severely censored in another. Accepted practices among children may be considered abnormalities in an adult population.

In many cases, when behavior transgresses the norm it should possibly be classed as cultural deviance rather than delinquency or criminality. As a youth, prior to his knowledge and acceptance of social mores and the law, deviations, while conceivable delinquencies, are probably not criminal. In old age, refusal to accept changing social expectations together with a rejection of the mores of the middle-aged population may bring the geronto into conflict with society. Such conflict may be considered delinquent behavior but not, in a majority of cases, truly criminal.

Delinquency in the gerontological population is difficult to determine and even more difficult to evaluate. Arresting officers tend to be excessively lenient to the older person (especially one well in excess of age 65) and will frequently "turn their backs" on certain offenses *unless the safety and/or rights of others are involved.* The drunk person and often one disturbing the peace in a minor way will be driven home or given a bed in jail for the night without being charged with any offense. Gambling, indecent exposure, vagrancy and driving under the influence are less frequently ignored, but leniency is still prevalent. Only in areas of "hard crime," e.g. aggravated assault, homicide, burglary, narcotics law violations, forcible rape, forgery and similar types of offenses, will the geronto, as a rule, be treated as would a younger person.

TABLE I

ARRESTS OF OLDER PERSONS
UNIFORM CRIME REPORTS—1969

Offense Charged	Urban		Rural		Total	
	60–64	65 & over	60–64	65 & over	60–64	65 & over
Drunkenness	65,244	54,492	1,953	1,607	67,197	56,099
Driving under the influence	8,270	5,257	1,180	921	9,427	6,178
Disorderly conduct	7,404	7,594	240	201	7,644	7,795
Gambling	3,414	4,227	184	179	3,598	4,406
Larceny-theft	2,900	3,553	79	82	2,979	3,634
Vagrancy	2,822	2,542	76	73	2,898	2,615
Liquor law violations	1,425	1,405	163	161	1,588	1,566
Aggravated assault	1,057	1,046	97	83	1,154	1,129
Carrying and possession of weapons	834	815	32	46	866	847
Sex offenses excepting rape and prostitution	547	693	39	38	613	712
Fraud	329	240	69	71	398	311
Offenses against family	215	141	45	41	260	182
Burglary	229	210	25	13	254	223
Narcotics law violations	203	193	3	5	207	198
Criminal homicide	178	233	23	36	201	259
Prostitution and commercialized vice	182	185	3	3	185	188
Vandalism	121	103	13	17	134	120
Forgery and counterfeiting	100	61	17	8	117	69
Auto Theft	54	52	4	2	58	56
Forcible Rape	30	28	1	9	31	37

Much information is available concerning crime in the United State in the *Uniform Crime Reports* issued each year by J. Edgar Hoover and the FBI. From this source we have prepared several tables. Table I shows the frequency of arrests for the twenty most frequently committed crimes perpetrated by those aged sixty to sixty-four and those sixty-five and over in rural and urban societies. Table II compares the frequencies of total arrests of those sixty-five and over in 1964 and 1969 in the same categories considered in Table I.

TABLE II

TOTAL ARRESTS OF PERSONS AGE 65 AND OLDER
UNIFORM CRIME REPORTS
1964–1969

Offense Charged	Total Arrests 1964	Total Arrests 1969	Change	Percent Change
Drunkenness	52,221	56,099	+3,878	+ 7%
Disorderly conduct	7,318	7,795	+ 477	+ 7%
Vagrancy	4,325	2,615	−1,710	− 39%
Driving under the influence	3,864	6,178	+2,314	+ 60%
Gambling	5,584	4,406	+1,178	+ 21%
Larceny	2,182	3,634	+1,452	+ 66%
Liquor law violations	1,954	1,566	− 388	− 20%
Aggravated assaults	885	1,129	+ 244	+ 28%
Sex offenses excluding rape and prostitution	843	712	− 131	− 16%
Carrying and possession of weapons	421	847	+ 426	+101%
Fraud	294	311	+ 17	+ 6%
Offenses against family	239	182	+ 56	+ 24%
Narcotics law violations	164	198	+ 32	+ 20%
Burglary	162	223	+ 61	+ 38%
Vandalism	161	120	− 41	− 25%
Prostitution and commercialized vice	135	188	+ 53	+ 39%
Criminal homicide	106	259	+ 153	+144%
Forgery and counterfeiting	95	37	− 7	− 16%
Auto theft	72	56	− 16	− 22%
Forcible rape	44	37	− 7	− 16%
Total arrests	81,068	86,624	+8,041	+ 10%

Material presented in these tables provides many frames of reference useful in evaluating delinquencies in the aged population. To get a true and useful picture, however, many additional frames not currently available must be provided.

It is interesting to know (see Table I) that 54,492 urban and 1,607 rural aged (65 and over) were arrested for drunkenness in 1969. It would be even more interesting to know what per cent of the total gerontological population is represented by this apparently large group. Is the actual percentage greater in urban or in rural areas? How many were arrested more than once during the year? More than five times? More than ten? How many were "sent home" when drunk instead of being arrested? Why do they drink? To escape loneliness? To forget? To regain their feelings of value and to enhance their self-concept? Do they drink alone or with others? If 56,099 were arrested, how many escaped punishment? Do members of the so-called upper classes drink more or less than do members of the lower classes? How do these two compare with the great middle class? Do the various ethnic groups and subcultures provide different statistical percentages of drunkenness? Only by conducting a comprehensive investigation of the drinking problems of the aged can we determine the significance of the fact than in 1969, 56,099 older persons were arrested for drunkenness.

A study of Table II will show a number of interesting and possibly significant changes. The fact that arrests for vagrancy declined by 39 per cent could indicate that the indigent are receiving better treatment from society and are many times, when necessary, being cared for in institutions. The 60 per cent increase in arrests on charges of driving while under the influence and the 21 per cent increase on charges of gambling could suggest a less lenient attitude on the part of arresting officers in these particular offenses.

A definite correlation must exist between the 101 per cent increase in arrests for carrying and possession of weapons, and the 38 per cent for burglary, the 28 per cent for aggravated assault, and the staggering rise of 144 per cent among those charged with criminal homicide. All are probably reflections of a changing social scene and the different attitudes presently held by the aged.

The 20 per cent increase in arrests for violations of the narcotics laws certainly relates to modern trends and to the fact that the gerontological generation is not too different from the average population—only older.

The Uniform Crime Reporting Program employs seven crime classifications to establish an index designed to measure the trend and distribution of crime in the United States. Offenses of murder, forcible rape, robbery and aggravated assault are categorized as violent crimes. Those of burglary, larceny ($50.00 and over) and auto theft are classed as crimes against property.

In Table III, we present a comparison of the incident of arrests for index crimes in 1964 with those in 1969 as committed by individuals sixty-five years of age and older.

Table IV presents another interesting picture of change. While

TABLE III

TOTAL ARRESTS OF PERSONS AGE 65 AND OLDER CHARGED WITH COMMISSION OF INDEX CRIMES

UNIFORM CRIME REPORTS
1964–1969

Violent Crimes

Offense Charged	Total Arrests 1964	Total Arrests 1969	Change	Percent Change
Homicide	106	259	+ 153	+144
Robbery	65	71	+ 6	+ 9
Forcible rape	44	37	− 7	− 16
Aggravated assault	885	1,129	+ 244	+ 28
Total violent crimes	1100	1,496	+ 396	+ 36
Crimes Against Property				
Burglary	162	223	+ 61	+ 38
Larceny ($50 & over)	2,182	3,634	+1,452	+ 67
Auto theft	72	56	− 16	− 24
Total property crimes	2,416	3,913	+1,497	+ 62
Total crime index	3,516	5,409	+1,893	+ 54

drunkenness and disorderly conduct increased only 7 per cent (little more than the increase in the older population), driving while under the influence swelled by a staggering 60 per cent and liquor law violations *decreased* by 20 per cent. Although types of violations of liquor laws are not specified, they are assumed to include unlawful sales, illegal manufacture and related violations.

TABLE IV

TOTAL ARRESTS OF PERSONS 65 AND OLDER CHARGED WITH DRUNKENNESS AND RELATED DELINQUENCIES

UNIFORM CRIME REPORTS
1964–1969

Offense Charged	Total Arrests 1964	Total Arrests 1969	Change	Percent Change
Drunkenness	52,221	56,099	+3,878	+ 7
Disorderly conduct	7,378	7,795	+ 477	+ 7
Driving under the influence	3,864	6,178	+2,314	+60
Liquor law violations	1,954	1,566	− 388	−20
Total Drunkenness and Related Delinquencies	65,357	71,638	+6,281	+10

The increase of driving under the influence may be traced to a variety of causes: more stringent laws, less lenient treatment of the aged in this category, more older people driving and different standards for determining drunken driving. Total arrests for drunkenness and related crimes increased only 10 per cent which, if we consider the 5.5 per cent increase in the total gerontological population, is minimal.

Table V has been prepared to reveal changes in sex crimes between 1964 and 1969. Sex offenses other than prostitution and rape (including homosexual violations, exhibitionism, voyeurism,

TABLE V

TOTAL ARRESTS OF PERSONS 65 AND OLDER CHARGED WITH SEX AND SEX RELATED CRIMES

UNIFORM CRIME REPORTS
1964–1969

Offense Charged	Total Arrests 1964	Total Arrests 1969	Change	Percent Change
Sex offenses excluding rape and prostitution	843	712	−131	−16
Prostitution and commercial vice	136	188	+ 53	+39
Forcible rape	44	37	− 7	−16
Total sex and related crimes	1,022	937	− 85	− 8

TABLE VI

ARREST TRENDS—TOTAL POPULATION

UNIFORM CRIME REPORTS
1964–1969

	Total Arrests 1964	Total Arrests 1969	Difference	Difference
	4,107,392	5,167,450	1,060,121	+26
Violent Crimes				
Homicide	8,222	12,883	4,661	+57
Forcible rape	8,463	12,499	4,036	+48
Robbery	36,566	67,290	30,724	+84
Aggravated assaults	73,389	96,945	24,556	+34
Total violent crimes	125,640	189,617	63,977	+51
Crimes Against Property				
Burglary	165,698	225,217	59,609	+36
Larceny (over $50)	316,670	467,166	150,498	+48
Auto theft	87,294	108,306	21,012	+24
Total property crimes	596,572	800,689	231,117	+41

Crimes				
Total Crime Index	695,212	990,306	295,094	+42
Other Significant				
Drunkenness	1,327,691	1,273,323	−54,368	− 4
Carrying and possession	42,512	81,609	39,097	+92
Driving under the influence	194,912	285,510	−90,518	−46
Total population of U.S.	192,000,000	202,710,000	10,710,000	+5.5
Total aged population	19,200,000	20,271,000	1,070,000	+5.5

TABLE VII

PERCENTAGE INCREASES IN ARRESTS
GERONTOS COMPARED TO TOTAL POPULATION

UNIFORM CRIME REPORTS
1964–1969
Percentage Increases in Crime
1964–1969

Offense	Total Population Percent of Increase	Gerontological Group Percent of Increase	Difference Percent
Violent Crimes			
Homicide	57	144	+ 87
Forcible rape	48	− 16	− 64
Robbery	84	9	− 75
Aggravated assault	34	28	− 6
Total violent crimes	51	36	− 15
Crimes Against Property			
Burglary	36	38	+ 2
Larceny	48	67	+ 19
Auto theft	24	− 24	− 48
Total property crimes	41	62	+ 21
Total Crime Index	42	54	+ 12
Other Significant Crimes			
Drunkenness	− 4	− 7	− 3
Carrying and possession of firearms	92	101	+ 9
Driving under the influence	−46	60	+106%

sadism, masochism, molesting, etc.) *decreased* by 16 per cent as did forcible rape. At the same time, prostitution *increased* by 39 per cent which may prove to be significant. It might be suggested that the availability of prostitutes makes it possible for the old to gain sexual satisfaction by safer means than rape. Rape victims of the old are usually children (of both sexes!) and older but subnormal persons. This is one area of crime among the aged where the arresting officers and the public at large refuse to be lenient. It may be that the public is becoming more tolerant of the behavior of the old with the old. A study in depth of the sex needs of the geronto seems to be sorely needed. How strong are their desires? What releases are available? What solutions are possible?

In order to determine the significance of the increase of arrests noted in the gerontological population, we must determine the increase in the total population. In Table VI will be found statistics concerning those felonies used in ascertaining the crime index together with three other significant crimes.

Table VII compares arrest statistics of the total population to those of the gerontological segment covering all crime index offenses together with three other significant categories. The percentages used are the changes between 1964 and 1969 reflecting increases or decreases in various classes of crime.

During the five-year period, older group arrests increased by 54 per cent while those of the total population were boosted by only 42 per cent. This shows a 12 per cent increase by the gerontos over the total population. In the violent crimes index, the total population increased over the older group by 15 per cent while in the property crimes index the older group led by 21 per cent.

In violent crimes, the oldsters led in only one category, homicide, where their increase was 87 per cent greater than that of the total population. The 64 per cent decrease in forcible rape and the 75 per cent decrease in robbery resulted in a 15 per cent decrease in the violent crimes index.

The gerontos show a 3 per cent decrease in drunkenness, a 9 per cent increase in carrying and possession of firearms, but a surprising 106 per cent increase in driving under the influence when compared with the total population.

Since the number of arrests of older Americans in 1969 is so small (56,099 for drunkenness being the largest category), just how important is the problem? From the total population of the United States in the same year, 1,273,323 (again the largest single category) were arrested on like charges. Since the total population in 1969 was 202,710,000, the number arrested on charges of drunkenness was .6 per cent as compared with .3 per cent of the 20,271,000 individuals sixty-five or over.

If we consider statistics drawn from the crime index, we find in 1969, 2.55 per cent of the total population charged with violations as compared with .43 per cent of the gerontological population. It would seem to appear that problems of delinquency among the older population are not too significant though the fact that even this many were discovered will be surprising to most individuals.

Even though the number of offenses was small and the per cent of the total aged population charged was insignificant, certain facts are suggestive. Among the seven crimes included in the crime index, percentage increases from 1964 to 1969 were noted in five. Only forcible rape and auto theft declined, the former by 16 per cent, the latter by 24 per cent. Most significantly, homicide increased by a staggering 144 per cent, larceny by 67 per cent and burglary by 38 per cent. Violent crimes in the index increased by 36 per cent, property crimes by 62 per cent with the total index showing a rise of 54 per cent. When the increase in the gerontological population over this five-year span was only 5.5 per cent, the rise in crime becomes most significant.

Answers to a number of significant questions must be provided before we can paint a true picture of gerontological delinquency and its causes. The hard statistics presented in the tables prepared for the first portion of this report will provide a point of departure for such an investigation. Among the questions to be answered:

1. How many arrested following their sixty-fifth birthday were first offenders.

2. How many can be classed as recidivistic?

3. When gerontos are habitual offenders, are offenses of identical nature?

4. At what age was the delinquent first apprehended?

5. Is delinquent behavior due primarily to psychopathic personality?

6. Is the delinquent behavior a product of psychogenic* disorders? somatogenic† psychosis?

7. Is the delinquent normal in all respects when clinically evaluated?

8. Is behavior a result of misdirected psycho-socio motivation?

With the continuing increase to be expected in the over sixty-five population, a study of delinquency and/or criminality appears almost mandatory. If the surge found in comparing the incident of arrests between 1964 and 1969 (percentage change, see Tables II, III, IV, V and VII) continues, a significant problem will develop in another ten years.

Presently, the information available concerning the delinquency of the gerontological population, while probably available in the records, has not been gathered together for study and evaluation. Before it would be possible to determine the significance of the apparent rise in offenses charged to the older persons, a study in depth must be conducted. Answers to the first four questions posed above are merely statistical and should be readily available from penitentiaries and reformatories. Answers to questions five, six and seven are a part of the inmate records in any institution where rehabilitation rather than punishment and the custodial function is the prime purpose behind commitment. Many other significant areas for evaluation would undoubtedly be discovered in a complete scrutiny of inmate records. The type of study suggested should be rather simple but might prove quite expensive. If the problem is as significant as it appears, however, it might be well worth any cost.

It is doubtful if many of the available records would indicate the true motivations underlying the delinquencies of the older American.

In most areas, there will be little change in the nature of motivation as one ages. Certain modification of direction and

---

*Impairment in psychological functioning with no known pathological change in organic structure and with assertion of a causal antecedent in the psychological history.

†Behavior patterns developed through metabolic changes in tissues or accidents.

intensity will, of course, occur. In addition, when a want or need has been completed and terminally satisfied, the motivating force activated by this need or want either disappears or becomes redirected. For example, the need for security tends to be one of the major psycho-socio motivating forces throughout life. When an individual reaches retirement he will, in a majority of cases, have achieved at least minimal security. Realizing that his position will change but little, he reconciles himself to his future and ceases to be motivated by any need for security. In a minimal number of cases where the individual refuses to accept his achieved level of security, the motivation will remain undiminshed but may be redirected. This redirection may be away from socially accepted practice and may actually lead to delinquency (larceny, forgery, fraud, burglary, etc.) in certain cases. In the event that an individual becomes delinquent in any of these areas *after* retirement and is arrested as a first offender, we may assume that redirection of the motive to achieve security may be considered a possible reason. With the recidivistic, it will undoubtedly be merely the continuation of a life style adopted in youth or young adulthood.

As a usual rule, the need to achieve status is not a strong motivating force in old age. Those who have attained an adequate level of prestige in earlier years may have terminally satisfied this particular drive. Others retain a halo of status in the post-retirement years that satisfies their need completely. A fairly small group of retirees who have never earned a "place in the sun" are continually motivated in old age. Many times these former non-achievers now obtain the status they need since those with whom they were required to compete have abdicated their social roles. Even when competing only with those who failed to achieve during their pre-retirement years, certain oldsters are still unable to fulfill their needs for status by socially acceptable means. If their need for prestige continues strongly, they may become delinquent, *just as do children and adolescents,* to build a feeling of importance. The individual may become a forger or commit fraud to enhance his personal feeling of superiority as he bilks another by his cunning. He may gamble, become a vandal, steal an auto or violate any number of statutes merely to satisfy his ego. At times he will tell friends and acquaintances about his activities to demonstrate his clever achievements.

Many gerontos become delinquent (just as do children) in their search for companionship. A number of footloose individuals with *nothing to do* may, regardless of age or sex, get into mischief that may be classed as criminal. Drunkenness, gambling, liquor law violations and vandalism are offenses that may be "companionship delinquencies."

Another possible, but infrequent, crime could be the use of narcotics or dangerous drugs. The sweet little old lady may be addicted to *uppers* or *downers* prescribed by a reputable physician. She may not be legally guilty of addiction despite the fact that any *young person* using the same quantities of identical dangerous drugs purchased in the black market would be considered delinquent. What exactly makes one use acceptable and another criminal? When the girls get together for bridge at a tenth of a cent a point, is this not gambling just as much as when men play poker or "shoot craps," regardless of stakes? Just what constitutes delinquency? Is delinquency evaluated in terms of where, when, why and how rather than in terms of the actual act? Or is delinquency only getting caught? In all probability, 90 per cent of all group misbehavior among the aged is either not apprehended or is ignored. Delinquency is not a matter of sex or age. The old transgress just as do the young, and females just as do males!

The single old person is far more apt to be caught in companionship delinquency than is the happily married individual or one living in an accepting home of children or other relatives. There is *never* any criminal intent in this type of violation, but merely an attempt to fill an empty life. An individual who commits an offense because of this pressing need should be warned and released. Nothing whatsoever will be gained by incarceration or by making the violation a matter of public knowledge. In almost every case, one warning would be enough to make the offender a model of decorum for all of his remaining days.

Chapter Fourteen

THE RETIREMENT SYNDROME

NO study of the psychological problems of the older American would be complete without an evaluation of retirement practices. Is retirement a result of aging or one of the prime causes? Or is it merely designed to permit employment of younger, often far less capable, *but cheaper,* individuals who "should have a chance to mature"?

What is sacrosanct about sixty-five or seventy or, for that matter, any other specific age? Does society ever consider that there are many who should be retired at forty-five or even forty due to senium praecox or to an early decline of quality in performance? Others may actually continue to improve into their eighties and even longer if permitted to remain in responsible positions.

It is often suggested that "young blood" is needed to provide new creative insights into continuing problems. Do the young have a monopoly on ideas? How will the unseasoned imagination of youth compare with the creativity based on experience frequently provided by oldsters? It would seem to this writer that a complete realistic appraisal of retirement practices must be made. If the custom of retirement at *any mandatory age* is to continue, better and far more realistic reasons must be provided if the retiree is to willingly accept termination of employment.

Government agencies, businesses and industry should be encouraged to cooperate on a study of retirement and the attendant problems. New criteria for superannuation could be developed in which age is not necessarily the prime factor. Is it not possible to evaluate performance and to base retirement time on effectiveness?

How many individuals develop psychological problems by being retained on the job when they are professionally and personally ripe for retirement? Probably just as many as develop similar problems from the post-retirement syndrome. Any society that can put men on the moon should be capable of designing an equitable retirement program which will be fair and beneficial to all concerned.

The prime argument against any plan to continue employment past age sixty-five is, of course, the supposition that such a practice would further glut the employment market. This would not be true if an effective plan based on logical criteria were to be developed. With proper implementation of a retirement practice based on effectiveness, performance and personal choice, there would be an almost equal number of persons who would retire before and after the magic age of sixty-five. Additional benefits would be noticed in the lessening of psychological problems not only among the retirees, but among the employed segment as well.

During the present century, the problem of retirement has become increasingly acute. Since 1907 the population of the United States has *more than doubled* and the percentage of individuals aged sixty-five and older has increased from 4.1 per cent to about 10.3 per cent. The cumulative effect of these changes is a *greater than fivefold* increase in the number of members of the society sixty-five and over. This rise in the number of older people reflects, of course, many factors, but regardless of causes, it has forced society into many new involvements.

Paralleling this surge in the population of the aged is an equally dramatic increase of children, preadolescents and preadults. The percentage has risen just as significantly in this group as in the gerontological population.

Since only so many employment opportunities are available in today's economy, decision must be reached concerning who shall work and who shall not. As a consequence, many more years of education and/or seasoning are required prior to complete acceptance into the work force. This tends to delay admission into competition with those already entrenched in industry, business and the professions. In many cases an individual is not accepted into any significant role in employment until age twenty-five or even thirty-five. By postponing the entry of the young and hastening the retirement of the old, an adequate balance between employment-unemployment is maintained, maintained at the expense of the young and the old! Can the same ends be gained by other means? A shorter work week? Fewer hours in the workday? Providing better service? Better professional care? These are questions which need consideration if many serious problems are to be prevented in the near future.

Individual reactions to retirement vary significantly in both direction and intensity. They will range between two extreme points on a continuum. Those at the far position on the left hate their work with a purple passion, dislike the very thought of going to the job each morning, watch the clock from 4:00 P.M. on in order to be ready to escape without an extra minute in bondage, distrust their fellow workers, have only contempt for their bosses, and always believe that they have far greater abilities than they can possibly use in their assigned responsibilities; these must be rated as barely adequate employees.

In contrast, those at the extreme right love every minute of every workday, can hardly wait to get started in the morning, refuse to believe that quitting time could possibly come so early in the day, find each new task a rewarding challenge, trust and personally like their co-workers, admire and respect their superiors, and, above all, receive intense satisfaction from their assigned tasks which are always completed impeccably. Only a few examples identical to either extreme type will be found. The distribution will probably conform rather well to the normal curve and we may expect to find about 7 per cent at each perfect extreme, 24 per cent who are very happy and 24 per cent equally unhappy with employment, and about 38 per cent who can be classed as completely indifferent to their work.

Basic reactions to retirement will probably be determined largely by job satisfaction, but will be tempered by a wide variety of psychological, sociological and economic factors. Those who were unhappy with their work but afraid to attempt a change because of a possible loss of security, will welcome retirement and vow that they will never again "turn a tap!" Unless other factors enter into the picture, this group will live out their lives (usually fairly long lives) in happy contentment. By contrast, those who have been happy with employment will resist retirement, maintaining that they have another ten or twenty years of competence left and will, when victims of mandatory separation, immediately start a search for fresh outlets for their talents. These are the unhappy victims of what they consider to be a senseless practice. Many times certain individuals will find a new niche and continue happy, productive lives for many years. This is the group who, when unable to find creative outlets, tend to live only a short time or to become senescent following retirement.

Those in the middle, indifferent group will be as unconcerned by retirement as they were apathetic to their work. Since they were never truly happy nor actually unhappy in employment, they will be lethargic in retirement. They will neither envy nor feel sorry for those who are still employed.

The prototypes described above are basic. A wide variety of factors will temper individual reactions and, as a result, no two persons will react to retirement in exactly the same manner. In all probability, only about 30 per cent to 35 per cent of all retirees will resent superannuation for other than money reasons. This group will come from among those who are truly happy with their life of employment. They bitterly resent laws and customs that entail retirement at any mandatory age. Given an option, many of these would retire at a *sensible* age voluntarily, but continue to resist what they believe to be an imposed mandate. The individuals in this group tend to be able, intelligent, well-educated, conscientious persons capable of making realistic assessments of their continuing abilities.

Given an option to remain on the job as long as they are able to perform at peak levels, these gerontos would, in a majority of cases, retire voluntarily when no longer completely effective. In the few cases where the worker refused to be realistic, a panel of his peers would determine when his time to retire has come. Using this plan, not only would many older Americans be permitted to remain in important posts, but many businesses, industries and institutions would profit greatly from their continuing superior contributions.

It seems just a bit idiotic to allow our laws to be made by legislators in their seventies and eighties, our health maintained by doctors well over sixty-five, our opinions molded by older writers and then to say that one at sixty-five is too old to remain in business, industry, education and many of the professions. What, other than an economic rationale could be used in determining the time of mandatory retirement?

As a result of untimely separation, many problems are generated for the 30 per cent to 35 per cent who resist retirement. Oftentimes an individual will develop neuroses and psychoses when he perceives himself as a social reject. His self-concept may be completely altered and his attitude toward society sterilized. His motivational levels tend to diminish, perceptual abilities dwindle from nonuse of the senses, his awareness subsides and his personality becomes ineffectual. He may avoid people and become introverted, even rejecting his family and former friends. As he develops feelings of inferiority and begins to perceive himself as being of doubtful value, his health deteriorates, his will to do dissipates and he becomes lethargic and a candidate for early senescence.

There are, of course, a number of ways to salvage this segment of the aged population. One excellent plan would be to retire the person at the mandatory age, but to retain him on the staff in an advisory or consulting capacity. He should be called on once or twice each month and paid adequately for his services. This would improve his financial position but far more importantly, should assist in preventing his sociopsychological disintegration.

A second solution could be the establishment of service agencies in communities to assist retirees in finding new and creative outlets for their abilities and talents. These agencies, headed by retired persons, could offer high-level, full or part-time services to business, industry and the agencies.

In addition to possible solutions which can be provided for the retiree, he has many personal options if he cares to exercise them. He may become self-employed using the expertise he has developed over the years or turn an avocation or hobby into a new vocation. In this type of endeavor, a certain amount of encouragement must be provided by others to help overcome the feelings of rejection and the changed self-concept which may have been engendered by retirement.

The truly capable, well-motivated, highly creative retired person should *never* be permitted by society to deteriorate until he either dies or becomes senescent. With just a little encouragement, many lives and talents can be salvaged and society could profit immeasurably.

Whether individual retirement is mandatory or voluntary, there are many problems that must be considered. The most significant (from the point of view of society) must, of course, be the economic, closely followed by the level of physical fitness necessary for continuing productive employment. These, the practical aspects, are more frequently considered in studies of retirement than are the basic personal problems involving the psychological factors which should also be deliberated. The practical are much more easily evaluated and have more social than personal relevance. As a result, only the psychologist or psychiatrist may have occasion to explore the results of the psychological trauma produced by retirement. Only in a few extreme cases will professional assistance be required despite the fact that all retirees are subject to some degree of psychic shock.

The individual who is unable to continue employment because of current policy or impaired health may find himself in an insecure position. Chief among his problems will probably be inadequate income. Unless he has been more farsighted than most, he will be required to exist on Social Security or company retirement, both of which tend to be inadequate. If he is unable to discover some field for self-employment, or be assisted in his search by some service agency, he will rather rapidly reach the end of his resources.

One destined to live out his life in want usually disintegrates, both physically and mentally. He may soon become debilitated and even develop an assortment of neuroses or become psychotic. His self-concept depreciates and he views himself as a social reject or, on his own initiative, becomes an isolate.

More important to many retirees than additional income is the *need to serve,* to be occupied and to remain in the mainstream of life. Important as money may seem to many, activity and involvement frequently prove to be more important. The older person who remains highly motivated will find outlets for his enterprise. The types of outlets will usually be determined by his life experiences, his remaining talents, his memory and maintained perceptual levels. His ability to adjust to new environments and new experiences will possibly dictate acceptable areas for involvement. If he hopes to work with people rather than things, his modified personality will prove an important factor in determining his potential for success. If any significant personality abnormalities have developed as a result of aging, new achievements will prove almost unattainable.

From birth to death, man plays various roles. Many have been identified and expectations established. The role of the child in our society has been rather completely defined as have those of many of the other developmental levels. The adult identifies with a variety of roles at one and the same time. A man may play the role of chief in his business or profession while he accepts a very minor role in the home and with the family. He will remain happy if he is able to adjust to each role and willingly accept his position, not only in his business and his home, but also in his church, service club, lodge and in every other relationship he enjoys.

When this person retires, almost every role is changed. He no longer has a business or profession, his consociations in the service and social clubs become less satisfying and many relationships dissipate completely. Only in the church and the home will little change be observed. This leaves the retiree in an almost complete state of noninvolvement. Unless this situation is remedied, the geronto will, because of psychosocial deprivation, tend to reject the society that purged him from his roles.

Either government or private enterprise should provide opportunities for the retiree to discover new roles designed to satisfy his basic need for involvement. When the geronto is in financial need, the role should, if possible, be a remunerative one. If the older person does not require financial assistance, his assignned role or roles could provide satisfaction, intellectual and/or emotional outlets, opportunities to serve and, above all, a chance to enhance his self-concept.

Substantially every problem inherent in retirement could be prevented by adequate pre-retirement education. This education should be provided long before retirement age since time is required to adequately prepare for separation from employment. Units in certain junior and senior high school courses could provide basic understandings which would not only launch personal preparation but also provide the young with better understandings of their grandparents' needs. Specific preparation for retirement should be started at least by age forty. Those who delay too long will not have the necessary time to equip themselves for the future.

A series of pre-retirement workshops should be provided for individuals *long* before they are to be superannuated. One week each year from age forty or forty-five until retirement should be devoted to preparation. Among subjects to be explored in the workshops, the following deserve consideration:

1. *Providing adequate income for the retirement years.* The pre-retired persons should be led to an understanding of the inadequacy of Social Security and/or company pensions. The various investments and savings plans that can be used to augment post-retirement income should be evaluated on an individual basis.

2. *The importance of friends in retirement.* The individual must be led to an understanding of the great need to cultivate many friends ten or fifteen years younger than self. If this is not done, the day will come when the retired person will have far more relatives than friends!

3. *The avocation which may become a new vocation.* All persons should develop a number of avocations that could conceivably change to new vocations on retirement. Those who discover that their incomes are inadequate may find some supplementation possible by new endeavors.

4. *Hobbies and peace of mind.* The pre-retired worker should be encouraged to become interested in one or more compelling hobbies. Since one of the major problems faced by the retiree is the great amount of leisure time, this becomes an important area of concern.

These are only suggestions to be used as guides in providing workshops. Many other areas such as politics, church and club activities, and volunteer services will provide additional types of acceptable activity.

The older person who is financially secure, able to utilize his free time constructively, happy in his social contacts and able to contribute services to others will find the later longevous period of life truly rewarding. He will retain a superior self-concept, remain highly motivated, rarely become neurotic or psychotic and live out his life happily. He will not suffer from psychosocial deprivation, nor will he become senescent. When one is adequately prepared for retirement, these may truly be the "golden years!"

SELECTED BIBLIOGRAPHY

Beatty, Ralph P.: *The Senior Citizen.* Springfield, Thomas, 1962.

Berezin, Martin A., and Cath, Stanley H.: *Geriatric Psychiatry.* New York, Int. Univs., 1965.

Bernadette de Lourdes, Mother: *Where Someone Cares.* New York, Putnam, 1959.

Birren, James E.: *The Psychology of Aging.* Englewood Cliffs, Prentice-Hall, 1966.

Blanchard, Fessenden Seaver: *Make the Most of Your Retirement: Where to Go, What to Do, How Much it Costs.* Garden City, Doubleday, 1963.

Botwinick, Jack: *Cognitive Processes in Maturity and Old Age.* New York, Springer, 1967.

Boyd, Rosamonde R., and Oaker, Charles G.: *Foundation of Practical Gerontology.* Columbia, University of South Carolina Press, 1969.

Bromley, Dennis Basil: *The Psychology of Human Aging.* Baltimore, Penguin, 1966.

Carp, Frances Merchant: *A Future for the Aged: Victoria Plaza and Its Residents.* Published for the Hogg Foundation for Mental Health. Austin, Austin, U. of Tex., 1966.

Chamber of Commerce of the United States of America: Task Force on Economic Growth and Opportunity: *Poverty: The Sick, Disabled, and Aged.* Washington, 1965.

Clark, Margaret, and Anderson, Barbara G.: *Culture and Aging: An Anthropological Study of Older Americans.* Springfield, Thomas, 1967.

Commerce Clearing House: *Medicare and Social Security Explained.* Chicago, 1965.

Conference on Medicine in Old Age, London, 1965: *Medicine in Old Age.* Philadelphia, Lippincott, 1966.

Council on Social Work Education: *Decision-making Process: A Case Illustration.* New York, 1964.

Curtis, Howard James: *Biological Mechanisms of Aging.* Springfied, Thomas, 1966.

Feingold, Eugene (Ed.): *Medicare; Policy and Politics. A Case Study and Policy Analysis.* San Francisco, Chandler Pub., 1966.

Garvin, Richard M.: *Where They Go to Die: The Tragedy of America's Aged.* New York, Delacorte, 1968.

Geist, Harold: *The Psychological Aspects of the Aging Process.* St. Louis, W. H. Green, 1968.

Handbook of Aging and the Individual, Psychological and Biological Aspects. Chicago, U. of Chicago, 1960.

Harris, Richard: *A Sacred Trust.* New York, New Am. Lib., 1966.

Hepner, Harry W.: *Retirement—a Time to Live Anew, a Practical Guide to Managing Your Retirement.* New York, McGraw, 1969.

Hersey, Jean: *These Rich Years: A Journal of Retirement.* New York, Scribner, 1969.

Hirschberg, Gerald G.: *Rehabilitation: A Manual for the Care of the Disabled and Elderly.* Philadelphia, Lippincott, 1964.

Hodkinson, Mary A.: *Nursing the Elderly.* Oxford, Pergamon, 1966.

Holtzman, Abraham: *The Townsend Movement. A Political Study.* New York, Bookman Associates, 1963.

Hopper, Langdon (Ed.): *Care of the Nursing-Home Patient.* Boston, Little, 1967.

Kalish, Richard (Ed.): *The Dependencies of Old People.* Ann Arbor, Institute of Gerontology, University of Michigan. Detroit, Wayne State U., 1969.

Koller, Marvin R.: *Social Gerontology.* New York, Random, 1969.

Lang, Gladys (Ed.): *Old Age in America.* New York, Wilson, 1961.

Larsen, Dorothy Hill: *Dialogues on Aging.* New York, Teachers College, 1966.

Lowenthal, Marjorie Fiske: *Aging and Mental Disorder in San Francisco: A Social Psychiatric Study.* San Francisco, Jossey-Bass, 1967.

Lucas, Carol: *Recreation in Gerontology.* Springfield, Thomas, 1964.

Malloy, Michael: *The Art of Retirement.* Silver Spring, Crown, 1968.

McKinney, John C. (Ed.): *Aging and Social Policy.* New York, Appleton, 1966.

Medevedev, Zhores Aleksandrovich: *Protein Biosynthesis and Problems of Heredity, Developing and Aging.* New York, Plenum, 1966.

Michigan University, Conference on Aging: *Aging and the Economy.* Ann Arbor, U. of Mich., 1963.

Milne, Lorus Johnson: *The Ages of Life; A New Look at the Effects of Time on Mankind and Other Living Things.* New York, Harcourt, 1968.

Moss, Bertram B.: *Caring for the Aged.* Garden City, Doubleday, 1966.

Neugarten, Bernice Levin: *Middle Age and Aging: A Reader in Social Psychology.* Chicago, U. of Chicago, 1968.
Newton, Kathleen: *Geriatric Nursing.* St. Louis, Mosby, 1960.
Niebanch, Paul L.: *Relocation in Urban Planning: From Obstacle to Opportunity.* Philadelphia, U. of Pa., 1968.
Physical Activity and Aging: With Special Reference to the Effects of Exercise and Training on the Natural History of Arteriosclerotic Heart Disease. Baltimore, University Park, 1970.
Pinner, Frank A.: *Old Age and Political Behavior: A Case Study.* Berkeley, U. of Calif., 1959.
Posman, Harry (Ed.): *Continuity in Care for Impaired Older Persons: Public Health Nursing in a Geriatric Rehabilitation and Maintenance Program.* New York, Department of Public Affairs, Community Service Society of New York, 1966.
Reichard, Suzanne Kate: *Aging and Personality: A Study of 87 Older Men.* New York, Wiley, 1962.
Reynolds, Frank Walker: *Adult Health: Services for the Chronically Ill and Aged.* New York, Macmillan, 1967.
Rosow, Irwing: *Social Integration of the Aged.* New York, Free Press, 1967.
Rubin, Isadore: *Sexual Life After Sixty.* New York, Basic Books, 1965.
Rudd, Thomas Newton: *The Nursing of the Elderly Sick: A Practical Handbook of Geriatric Nursing.* Philadelphia, Lippincott, 1954.
Schwartz, Doris R.: *The Elderly Ambulatory Patient: Nursing and Psychosocial Needs.* New York, Macmillan, 1954.
Shanas, Ethel: *The Health of Older People. A Social Survey.* Cambridge, Harvard, 1962.
Smith, Ethel: *The Dynamics of Aging.* New York, Norton, 1956.
Social Casework: *Casework with the Aging.* New York, Family Service Assn., 1961.
Sommers, Herman Miles: *Medicare and the Hospitals, Issues and Prospects.* Washington, Brookings, 1967.
Spiegelman, Mortimer: *Ensuring Medical Care for the Aged.* Published for the Pension Research Council, Wharton School of Finance and Commerce, University of Pennsylvania. Homewood, Ill., Irwin, 1960.
Symposium on the Family, Intergenerational Relations and Social Structure, Duke University, 1963: *Social Structure and the Family: Generational Relations.* Englewood Cliffs, Prentice-Hall, 1965.
Symposium on Topics in the Biology of Aging, San Diego, California, 1965: *Topics in the Biology of Aging.* New York, Interscience, 1966.

Talland, George A.: *Human Aging and Behavior: Recent Advances in Research and Theory.* New York, Academic, 1968.

Thewlis, Malford Wilcox: *The Care of the Aged (Geriatrics),* 6th ed., St. Louis, Mosby, 1954.

Tibbitts, Clark (Ed.): *Aging in Today's Society.* Englewood Cliffs, Prentice-Hall, 1960.

Townsend, Peter: *The Family Life of Old People: An Inquiry in East London.* London, Routledge and K. Paul, 1957.

Verzar, F.: *Lectures on Experimental Gerontology.* Springfield, Thomas, 1963.

Ware, George Whitaker: *The New Guide to Happy Retirement.* New York, Crown, 1968.

Wasser, Edna (Comp.): *Casebook on Work with the Aging.* New York, Family Service Assn., 1966.

Weiss, James: *Nurses, Patients and Social Systems: The Effects of Skilled Nursing Intervention Upon Institutionalized Older Patients.* Columbia, U. of Mo., 1968.

Welford, Alan Traviss, and Birren, James E.: *Behavior, Aging, and the Nervous System: Biological Determinants of Speed of Behavior and Its Change With Age.* Springfield, Thomas, 1965.

Williams, Arthur Milton: *Recreation in the Senior Years.* New York. Assn. Pr., 1962.

Williams, Richard Hays: *Lives Through the Years: Styles of Life and Successful Aging.* New York, Atherton, 1965.

Youmans, E. Grant (Ed.): *Older Rural Americans: A Sociological Perspective.* Lexington, U. of Ky., 1967.

Appendix A

A PORTRAIT OF THE OLDER AMERICAN

Mark Twain once said, "The trouble with many people is that they know so much that ain't so." Never has this been so perfectly demonstrated as in the accepted concept of the old. Ask the man-on-the-street to describe a typical older American and he will say, "The old person is ill, unable to make his own decisions, helpless, poor and . . ." This is, of course, the accepted stereotype, but a recent study of 159 randomly selected individuals between sixty-five and one hundred and one provides a completely different picture. With the sincere hope that a new stereotype may result, this portrait is presented for consideration.

The typical geronto is either married or a widow/widower who lives in his own home or in an apartment. His income is in the "low-but-adequate" income range. Those in a more comfortable financial position tend to have two or more sources of funds which may include company pensions, annuities, dividends, interest and/or cash reserves.

Many gerontos who have been retired would like employment. It seems that a hierarchy of factors which are collectively but not individually significant determine the desire to be employed. Financial need seems the least important factor while satisfaction realized in pre-retirement employment appears most significant. Those who retired voluntarily less frequently wish to return to the work force than do those whose retirement was mandatory. A desire to contribute to society is another pertinent factor in the hierarchy.

The average older American remains quite active. At least one-half of the over sixty-six population could and should be a part of the work force. Only a very small percentage are completely inactive with a majority of this small segment handicapped. In addition, a very high level of personal independence may be observed. At least 75 per cent of the older group are completely independent while those who require assistance need help only in minor specific areas such as transportation.

Hypochondria is no more prevalent with the over sixty-five than with the younger adult population. Even when investigators consider the subjects to be chronically ill, they personally feel their condition to be either good or fair. In this study of 159 aged persons, *only* 3.9 per cent reported their condition to be poor. The geronto deems illness "something to tolerate," feels it to be a "part of living," or considers it "only a bother."

The self-concept held by the older person is probably almost identical to the evaluation of worth accepted as a younger adult. Feelings of inferiority are not, as usually believed by the uninformed, typical of the aged. The small sample (less than 10 %) who consider themselves inferior probably reflect opinions conceived during youth or the middle years.

"Teenagers and their ways," "intolerance and prejudice" and "not getting things done" are the factors which annoy the gerontological population more than any others. Individuals seventy and over have fewer irritations than those between sixty-five and seventy. The stereotyping of the older persons as more crabby, contentious, fault-finding, abnormally irritable or easily annoyed than a younger sample cannot be substantiated. While areas of annoyance may change and personal responses heighten, the percentage of irritated, annoyed individuals will *not* increase with age.

The old maintain a strong interest in society with nearly one-half involved and another quarter passively interested. Only a very small percentage (probably those who were social isolates or rejects in their younger years) fail to express any interest. Females under seventy indicate "scant interest" more frequently than any group but, despite this fact, one-third remain involved.

Closely related to the above are the opinions of the gerontos concerning the state of the world today. Not surprising is the fact that 42.1 per cent state categorically that the world is worse today than twenty years ago. On the other hand, few individuals would anticipate that 27 per cent believe the world to be better today, 7.5 per cent believe it is better in many ways while 17 per cent see no particular change. Evaluations of the behavior patterns of the young tend to parallel opinions concerning the status of the world. Almost one-half are critical while an equal number are supportive. Among the aged, the most critical group are the females seventy and older while the females under seventy are the most tolerant.

Contrary to expectations, little relationship exists between goals set in youth and attitudes toward religion. Well over half of the aged describe themselves as being very religious but only a small percentage have had as their goal in life "service to the Lord!" Actually, the two prime goals were "to succeed in a career" and "to be a good spouse and parent."

A majority of the gerontos would change nothing in their lives if they could live them over again. Modifications others would make involve change of occupation or change of marriage. Males under seventy would most frequently change occupations while the under-seventy female would change her marriage more often.

The most startling opinions of the old concern the so-called sex revolution. More than one-third express *no condemnation* while many note that there are few changes in *actual sex practice* but that more honesty and forthrightness may be observed today. Females under seventy express more permissive acceptance, while females seventy and over and both categories of males agree that modern sex practices are bad.

In the gerontological years, motivational change must be expected. An increase in the felt need for security is frequently expressed but not to the degree one would expect. Males over seventy are most secure while females under seventy show anxiety. Other motivational forces which lose impetus include need for status and a variety of hedonistic impulses.

An assessment of the value judgments of the aged concerning Social Security and Medicare provide some interesting facts. Generally, Social Security is considered to be good but, in too many cases, not completely adequate. The same group, on the other hand, are disenchanted with Medicare. While Social Security is well-established and understood by the recipients, Medicare appears bewildering. In addition, unless the individual has the medical insurance supplement and/or commercial insurance as well, his coverage will be completely inadequate. It is interesting to know that a very small number of persons consider these federal programs a *step towards socialism!*

The gerontos believe that there are a number of advantages in growing old. Added "free time," "fewer responsibilities," "time to think" and "time to enjoy the family" are frequently mentioned. Other suggestions include "no further need to impress others," a "diminishing need for status" and "escape from the rat race." When asked to suggest disadvantages, those most frequently cited include "loss of sexuality and the debilitating body."

Appendix B

THE NONPATHOLOGICAL GERONTO

During the 1969–1970 academic year, 170 individuals between the ages of sixty-five and one hundred and one were assessed in a project sponsored by the Southern Colorado Gerontological Institute. Assessments were made by students, relatives, friends and by professionals including social workers, nurses, medical doctors and psychologists. All of the evaluators were oriented by the director of the institute to assure some level of uniformity in individual reports. Eleven cases were not used due to inconsistencies or, in a few instances, incomplete reporting. The total study is based, then, on 159 cases selected at random in order to obtain an unbiased sample.

As a result of the random selection, the sample contains a rather normal distribution in terms of the total population with fewer than 10 per cent of the respondents belonging to the pathological segment. The pathological group is considered, in this study, to be made up of the geriatric (chronically ill), the senescent (those losing their mental faculties) and the indigent gerontos.

Twenty-five subjects were studied in Lewiston, Idaho, twelve in Kansas, ten in Texas, four in Wyoming and the balance in Colorado, primarily Pueblo and Pueblo County.

The 159 evaluations were of forty-five males seventy and over and twenty-one under seventy with sixty-six females seventy and over and twenty-seven under seventy. The breaking point, seventy, was selected to divide the group into one sample (111 cases) born during the nineteenth century and one (48 cases) born during the twentieth. Females, ninety-three, outnumbered males, sixty-six, by about the proportion found in the total population of the elderly.

The total sample included 45.28 per cent who were married, 45.9 per cent widows or widowers with 1.88 per cent single and

6.92 per cent divorced. Only three individuals (1 male and 2 females) had never married. Of the eleven who were divorced, eight were females and six of these were under seventy. Widows outnumbered widowers sixty to thirteen while among the respondents still living with a spouse, men outnumbered women forty-nine to twenty-three. These facts merely reflect the expected longevity of the sexes and the probability that husbands are older than their wives.

One-hundred-twenty-six (79%) of the total sample live in their own homes and seventeen (10.69%) in apartments. This would tend to authenticate the sample as being nonpathological as would the fact that only thirteen (8.18%) are institutionalized or in nursing homes. Married subjects and widows/widowers live in private homes or apartments in substantially all cases as do those who are divorced. Those few individuals in institutions and nursing homes come from all categories except the divorced. On the basis of these findings, one may safely say that 90 per cent of the gerontological population are self-sufficient to the point that they can live rather independent lives.

A majority of the respondents have either moderate (47.79%) or low-but-adequate (42.14%) incomes. Only 5.66 per cent are well-to-do and 4.40 per cent indigent or living at a bare subsistence level. The well-to-do come largely from the seventy and older group and are equally divided between male and female.

Those with low-but-adequate incomes must curtail their spending and restrict their activities but do tend to be self-sufficient. With 95.59 per cent of the total sample above the bare subsistence income level, it would seem that the nonpathological population of older citizens tends to be financially independent.

In 82.4 per cent of the cases, the individual controls his own resources while in 8.1 per cent the spouse becomes the manager. Finances are administered by children, relatives, guardians or agencies for only 9.5 per cent of the group.

In the total sample, 70 per cent indicate their primary source of income to be Social Security or railroad retirement. The well-to-do segment generally report annuities or interest and dividends to be the main source of revenue. While the two cases reported as indigents and the five on bare subsistence income are receiving

Appendix

Social Security, the solitary individual on welfare is considered to have a low-but-adequate income.

The well-to-do usually receive income from three or more sources; the moderate income segment from at least two. Some maintain significant bank balances to augment total income as needed.

The individuals in the low-but-adequate category either have maximum Social Security or lesser income from this source augmented by supplements. Those with minimal Social Security only are not in good financial position.

One might well expect a close relationship to exist between the financial position of the individual and his positive desire to be employed, but statistics do not verify the expectation. While 24.5 per cent of the moderate income group would like to be employed only 17.6 per cent of those in the bare subsistence category expressed a similar desire. In addition, though the sample is too small to be significant, twice as many of the well-to-do as those on a bare subsistence income wish to work. The single indigent in the sample prefers not be to employed.

It would seem that factors other than financial need determine the desire of individuals over sixty-five to have jobs. A large majority, 68.6 per cent, of the under-seventy sample of retirees who *were happy in their pre-retirement employment* would like to have jobs while only 25 per cent prefer a life of leisure. With the seventy and older group, desires are somewhat different: 34.2 per cent would like employment but 42.3 per cent would not. Only 18.3 per cent of the total sample of 159 individuals stated that they were not happy with their pre-retirement occupation; 1.9 per cent would like to be employed but 16.4 per cent would not. With *mandatory retirement*, 10.7 per cent of the total sample were happy while 27 per cent were not. On the other hand, when retirement was voluntary, 39 per cent were happy as contrasted with only 4.4 per cent who were not. Interestingly, 18.9 per cent are not as yet retired.

It would seem that the desire to be employed after age sixty-five may be related to a hierarchy of factors which are collectively but not individually significant. Of the total sample, 46.6 per cent wish to be employed. Of this group, virtually all were happy in their pre-retirement occupation and a major percentage of the individuals were victims of mandatory retirement. These two factors are apparently more significant than the financial position of the individual.

The level of activity of the subjects provides additional insights concerning the post-retirement needs of the older American. With 20.1 per cent very active and 24.5 per cent active, we find 44.6 per cent who are not interested in a sedentary existence. Another 6.9 per cent hold part-time jobs, and 5 per cent hold full-time jobs. Thus, well over one-half of the subjects *should* be a part of the work force. The 15.7 per cent who do their own housework and the 8.8 per cent who garden and "take walks" are probably quite happy to be active but unemployed. Only 6.2 per cent of the 159 subjects are not active. These individuals would, even though interested, probably be unable to accept employment.

It is a generally accepted fact that the older American feels himself to be dependent on others. Thus, another fallacy coming from preoccupation with the stereotypic 10 per cent is completely refuted in this study, with 74.2 per cent of the entire group reporting that they feel themselves to be *completely* independent in every respect. In 1.3 per cent of the cases, the respondent depends on the spouse and in 1.9 per cent is independent save in the area of transportation. While 13.2 per cent report that they are "not too independent," *not one admits to being completely dependent.*

Hypochondria is no more prevalent with the over sixty-five than with the younger adult population. Even when investigators considered the subject to be chronically ill, they personally appraised their condition as either good or fair. Only 3.9 per cent of the total sample reported their condition as poor while 25.9 per cent were evaluated by the investigators as being chronically ill, showing weakness from old age, or being senile. Attitudes expressed toward illness are quite interesting: 44.6 per cent "tolerate illness," 20.1 per cent feel it to be a "part of living," and 24.5 per cent consider it "only a bother."

Feelings toward death are similar to those towards illness with 64.8 per cent of the sample professing no fear while another 7.5

per cent maintain that they consider mortality in the Christian context. Thus, a total of 72.3 per cent face the future without expressed apprehension. Only 6.3 per cent state that they fear death but another 8.8 per cent refuse to discuss the inevitable. A total, then, of 15.1 per cent seem to have some level of anxiety concerning their future. No significant correlation can be discovered between self-evaluation of health and attitudes toward death.

Despite the fact that the amount of time (between 12 and 15 hours) spent with each subject was inadequate, the investigators attempted to evaluate the self-concept held by each individual. These evaluations were correlated with "feelings of worth" as expressed by the respondents. Of the 75.5 per cent of the subjects who feel themselves to be worthwhile, 41.5 per cent were evaluated as having a very good self-concept, 8.2 per cent as self-sufficient, 6.9 per cent as average or better, 10.1 per cent as still having purpose with only 3.8 per cent as having limitations and 5 per cent as being helpless or useless. Of the 15.7 per cent who considered themselves of "some worth," 4.4 per cent were evaluated as having a "very good" self-concept, 2.5 per cent as "self-sufficient," 3.1 per cent as "average or better," 1.9 per cent "still has purpose," 2.5 per cent "has limitations," and 1.3 per cent "useless-helpless." This leaves only a negligible sample (under 10%) who feel of "no worth." It would seem that the relationship between these two factors tends to authenticate them both.

The older citizens as a group are stereotyped as being crabby, contentious, fault-finding, abnormally irritable and easily annoyed. The data accumulated in this study does not substantiate this view. Generally, members of this group have about the same number of annoyances that would be expected in any younger sample. While 24.5 per cent of the total sample indicate few irritations, there were some differences in the age and sex groups. Males over seventy, in 31.1 per cent of the cases, report few irritations but males under seventy seem more susceptible with 19 per cent reporting irritations. The converse is found among the females, the under-seventy group reporting 25.9 per cent and those over seventy, 22.9 per cent. It is surprising to find, in this sample, that the seventy and over population have fewer irritations (25.2%) than do those under seventy (22.9%).

"Teenagers and their ways" are reported as the most irritating factor to males seventy and over (28.8%), to females seventy and over (15.1%) and one of three disturbing factors to males under seventy (18.5%). To the males under seventy "intolerance and prejudice" is, in 42.8 per cent of the cases, the most annoying element. In order of frequency with the total sample of expressed areas of annoyance, we find the following:

1	Teenagers and their ways	20.1%
2.	Intolerance and prejudice	18.2%
3.	Not getting things done	11.9%
4.	Helplessness	9.4%
5.	Being alone	5.7%
6.	Drinkers	4.4%
7.	War	3.8%
8.	Working mothers	1.9%

It is interesting to identify categories where specific annoyances are expressed. Drinkers (in this study) annoy only females and most especially those seventy and over. Working mothers irritate only females seventy and over. Being alone annoys males and females over seventy, but women more than men.

If the youth of this generation were to be canvassed, their greatest source of annoyance would be war, but in the gerontological sample war ranks *seventh* out of *eight* factors and is mentioned by only 3.8 per cent of the respondents.

Only two categories are cited by the subjects that tend possibly to be unique to a gerontological sample—helplessness and being alone. While other age groups may contain those who are annoyed by these problems it will be a minimal number. In the age group under study, 15.1 per cent find helplessness and being alone to be significant sources of discomfort.

It is frequently suggested that the older American has a negligible interest in society. The material gathered in this study tends to refute this idea, for 46.5 per cent of the total sample apparently have an involved interest and 27 per cent passive interest. While 12.6 per cent express specific concerns, only 13.8 per cent failed to express any interest whatsoever in society.

Females seventy and over indicate "little social interest" in 21 per cent of their sample to lead all groups in this category. Despite this fact, 33.2 per cent are still "much involved" and 28.7 per cent express at least "passive concern." Surprisingly, the largest percentage of involvement, 62.9 per cent, and the smallest of "little interest," 37 per cent, are found in the female under-seventy group.

Generally, the total sample under seventy tends to be more involved in social activities than the older group and to have fewer individuals expressing scant interest.

Stated opinions concerning the present status of the world relate rather closely to previously expressed sentiments. Not at all surprising is the belief expressed by 42.1 per cent of the total sample that the world is worse today than it was twenty years ago. On the other hand, few individuals would have expected 27 per cent to believe it to be better, 7.5 per cent better in some ways and 17 per cent neither better nor worse. Thus, 51.5 per cent of the sample do not condemn society but tend to give tacit support to change, 3.1 per cent expressed no opinion and 3.1 per cent (interestingly, *all ladies*) stated that the world is now more exciting.

Evaluations of the behavioral patterns of the young by the gerontos tend to parallel opinions concerning the present status of the world. While 3.1 per cent of the total sample believe that the young are "going to pot," 18.9 per cent maintain that they are too wild. Surprisingly, 24.5 per cent make no specific evaluations but merely state that teenagers have "too many freedoms." Another 24.5 per cent find the young "interesting." Two individuals (both ladies over 70) believe them to be religious and 21.4 per cent find no real reason for criticism. Thus, 22 per cent specifically believe the behavioral patterns of the young merit criticism while 22.7 per cent believe the contrary to be true. It is, of course, impossible to determine how the young are evaluated by those who feel they have too many freedoms and those who find them interesting. One might postulate that 50 per cent of each group would be critical and 50 per cent supportive. Were this true, we would have 46.5 per cent critical of youth, 47.2 per cent supportive, and 6.3 per cent expressing no opinion.

The most critical group is composed of the females seventy and older where 33.2 per cent expressed criticism of today's youth. The most tolerant group are the females under seventy with only 7.4 per cent captious. The most tolerant group, females under seventy, find no valid reason for criticism. As one might expect, females over seventy are the least permissive with 15.1 per cent.

While supportive statistics are not available, the writer would suggest empirically that this age group seems somewhat less critical of the young than do the middle-aged. This is due largely to the fact that grandparents are, generally, more permissive than are parents.

Contrary to expectations very little relationship exists between goals set in youth and attitudes toward religion expressed by older Americans. Each factor seems independently significant, but only a very tenuous correlation can be discovered.

Attitudes Toward Religion In Rank Order

1. Active Christian	40 —	25.2%
2. Quite religious	38 —	23.9%
3. Sees value in religion	23 —	17.6%
4. Religion is the purpose for living	20 —	12.6%
5. Ignores religion	15 —	9.4%
6. Religion is too restricting	9 —	5.7%
7. Religion is alright	6 —	3.8%
8. A recent interest	3 —	1.9%

In at least ninety-eight cases (61.3%), respondents describe themselves as being *very* religious while in only twenty-four cases (15.1%) are subjects nonreligious. While supporting statistics are not available, it is doubtful if 10 per cent of the young in today's society would profess any religious conviction whatsoever.

Rank Order of Goals Set in Youth

1. To succeed in a career	62 —	39.0%
2. To be a good spouse and parent	56 —	35.0%
3. To live a good life and help others	20 —	12.6%
4. No goals established	15 —	9.4%
5. To serve the Lord	6 —	3.8%

These goals are probably not too dissimilar from those established by the young adults in this generation. The rank order would, however, be quite different. Many of today's youth feel that career success is a goal of the establishment and they reject this as a prime ambition. Service to others, however, becomes *very* important to members of the new generation who have developed a keen social conscience.

It is surprising that when 61.3 per cent of the total sample professed to being very religious, only 3.8 per cent dedicated their lives to serving the Lord. Of this "dedicated" group, 22.6 per cent selected the more practical goal of success in a career. Other established ambitions (to be a good spouse and parent and to live a good life and help others) expressed by 33.4 per cent of the professing Christians tend to relate more positively.

Responses to a question concerning the "sex revolution" provide possibly the most startling information reported in this study. Amazingly, 37.1 per cent of the total sample expressed no condemnation of modern sex practices. A number of respondents noted that actual practice had changed little but that, today, honesty and forthrightness have replaced secrecy and equivocation.

Females under seventy express the most permissive attitudes with 59.1 per cent either approving or finding no fault with current sex practices. Interestingly, the over-seventy males (28.8%) and the over-seventy females (28.7%) are in almost complete agreement in sanctioning the sex revolution. A slightly higher percentage of females over seventy than of males in the same age group (58.9% vs. 44.4%) state categorically that the modern attitudes toward sex are bad. The older sample, raised by mid-Victorian parents, tend to be more conservative (even prudish!) than the younger group nurtured in less restrictive environments.

One-half of the older persons studied in the project stated that if they could live their lives over they would not change a single thing! This degree of satisfaction with life is surprising. Vocational (20.7%) and marriage (10.7%) changes were most frequently mentioned by the dissatisfied. Only 3.9 per cent would have changed their entire lives while 3.1 per cent would take better care of themselves.

The largest percentage signifying that they would change their marriage, 28.6 per cent, was found in the female under-seventy group and the smallest, 7.5 per cent, in the female over-seventy sample. Little difference was found between the male samples where 9.5 per cent over and 8.8 per cent under seventy would change their marriage. Of males under seventy, 33.3 per cent would change occupations as contrasted with only 11.1 per cent of the seventy and over group. There is less spread among the females with 28.6 per cent versus 22.6 per cent.

As an individual moves into the gerontological years, changes in personal motivation are to be expected. Certain forces considered important during youth and the mature years may no longer remain significant while others are intensified. One of the prime motives throughout life is the search for security.

In the present study, 52.2 per cent of the subjects indicates a greater need for security in old age while 20.8 per cent feel less need and 24.5 per cent indicate no change. One surprising factor may be the statistics that in the over-seventy sample, 24.3 per cent indicate that they feel less need for security today, while the under-seventy group agreed in only 12.5 per cent. Males over seventy, with 33.3 per cent indicating less need, seem the most self-sufficient group while females under seventy, 11.1 per cent, appear the least secure.

In all probability, the most significant fact to be discovered in this area of investigation is that there is *not a great increase* in felt need for security in the gerontological population.

A study of the value judgments of the respondents towards Social Security and Medicare educed some interesting facts. While 60.3 per cent of the seventy and older sample find the programs to be acceptable or positively support them, only 45.9 per cent value the programs most highly, while males under seventy agree in only 28.5 per cent of their sample.

Generally, males under seventy feel that the programs do help but are inadequate. This response in 52.4 per cent of the cases is double that of the total sample where agreement is found in only 25.2 per cent of the responses.

It is not surprising that a larger percentage of the total sample who are happy with Social Security are disenchanted with Medicare. Social Security is well-established and well-understood by the recipients. On the other hand, Medicare is difficult for the old to understand and, unless the individual has the insurance supplement and some other program as well, these resources will usually prove inadequate.

It is amusing to note that four cases, 2.5 per cent of the total, all females, believe that these programs are a *step towards socialism!*

When asked if there were advantages in growing old, 59.2 per cent could list a number despite the fact that 32.7 per cent declared there were none. While 22 per cent felt that the added "free time" was an advantage, 21.4 per cent listed "fewer responsibilities" as being of importance. Only 8.8 per cent appreciated the extra time to enjoy their families while 4.4 per cent found "more time to think" a distinct advantage. While 89.7 per cent of the sample responded to this question (11.3% did not answer), to a companion question, "What are the advantages of growing old," only 15.1 per cent reacted. No conclusions could be drawn from this completely inadequate sample. The writer has searched for possible reasons for the limited number of responses to this question, but has been unable to discover any satisfactory answers.

This abstract presents the salient features of the study and provides the reader with what may be considered an atypical view of the older American. The complete study is available to interested individuals from the secretary of the Institute.

GLOSSARY

catharsis. The purification or purging of emotions. The release of tension and anxiety by emotionally reliving the past, or by any other satisfying experience.
centenarian. One who is 100 years old (or in his 100's).
concomitant. Accompanying, conjoined, attending. That which accompanies.
congruence. Superposable so as to be coincident. Points of agreement.
cps. Cycles per second.
debilitating. Enfeebling, weakening.
developmental periods, *(1) later maturity.* The first segment of the gerontological period from fifty-eight through sixty-eight. *(2) early longevous.* The middle portion of the gerontological period from sixty-eight through seventy-eight. *(3) later longevous.* The final portion of the gerontological period from seventy-eight until death.
DNA. Deoxyribonucleic acid. The complex molecules of which genes are composed. DNA is thought to be the mechanism for genetic inheritance.
ESP. Extrasensory perception—a response to an external event not presented to our known sense, from without the senses.
euphoria. A mood or emotional attitude of "all is well."
geriatric. Having to do with elderly people and with old age. *Usual connotation today,* "one who is old, ill, and physically incapacitated."
geriatrician. A doctor who practices in the field of geriatric medicine (geriatrics).
geronto. Old man, old person, old age.
gerontocracy. Government by the old.
gerontological period. That period of time from the later middle years until death. Roughly from age fifty-eight.
gerontologist. One who studies the problem of the aged and/or one who works with the older nonpathological geronto.
gestalt. A form, a configuration, or a totality that has, as a unified

---

All definitions in this glossary are taken either from *A Comprehensive Dictionary of Psychological and Psychoanalytical Terms* by English and English, or from *Webster's Seventh New Collegiate Dictionary.*

Glossary

whole, properties which cannot be derived by summation from the parts and their relationships.

ghetto. Housing prescribed for and restricted to a particular group.

ghettoize. To house in a ghetto.

hedonism. Psychological doctrine that every act is motivated by the desire for pleasure or the avoidance of unpleasure.

hypothalamus. A group of nuclei at the base of the brain involved in most visceral regulative processes.

liminal. Upper and/or lower limits. Thresholds.

longevity. The span of life.

longevous. Long-lived.

milieu. Environment, setting.

nonogenarian. One who is ninety years old (or in his 90's).

obdurate. Hardened in feeling; unyielding, hardhearted.

overtone. Sound produced by sympathetic vibration as a part of a fundamental tone.

onerous. Burdensome, oppressive, imposing a burden.

partial. Any one of the component pitches that make up a musical tone.

predisposition. A gene-determined characteristic favoring the devolpment or acquisition of a certain trait or quality. Any tendency to dispose of or determine beforehand.

presbycusis. The deterioration of auditory receptors resulting in the loss of the capacity to respond to the higher frequencies of sound.

presbyopia. A defect of vision which comes with advancing age due primarily to the hardening of the lens.

prosthetic. An artificial device to replace a missing or nonfunctioning part of the body, e.g. dentures, eyeglasses.

recidivistic. The tendency to repeat delinquent or criminal conduct or the recurrence of a mental disorder.

reticular formation. The formation of the brain consisting of small clumps of cell bodies or gray matter embedded in fibers.

RNA. Ribonucleic acid. Complex molecules that are believed to act as transfer agents and messengers in genetic development. May be important in memory storage.

senile. Of, pertaining to, exhibiting or characteristic of old age. *Usual connotation,* "having lost mental capabilities."

senescence. The period during which an individual lives as a senescent. The fact or condition of being senescent.

senescent. Growing old, aging. *Usual connotation today,* "One who is old, losing his mental capacities, unable to make own decisions."

septuagenarian. One who is seventy years old (or in his 70's).

sociopath. A person who is hostile and aggressive toward society or social institutions.

somatosensory. Through the body senses.

superannuation. Retirement or pension because of old age.

threshold. The statistically determined point at which a stimulus is just barely adequate to elicit a particular organismatic response.

INDEX

A
Adustment, 7, 10, 23, 26, 41, 42, 43, 47, 75, 87, 88, 89, 93, 95, 96
Affiliation, 24, 48
Agitation, 110
Anxiety, 88, 105
Arteriosclerosis, 110, 119
Attitudes, 26, 60, 87, 91
Avocations (hobbies), 18, 19, 53, 59
Awareness, 77, 78, 79, 81

B
Bio-chemical change, 82
Blair, A. W., 9f
Burbank, Luther, 29
Burton, W. H., 9f

C
Casals, Pablo, 29
Climacteric, male, 12
Compensation, 27
Creativity, 28, 29
Criteria of reality, 34

D
Debilitation, 11, 14, 37, 38, 51, 63, 67, 76, 92
Decision making, 35
Delinquency, 120, 122, 123, 128, 131
Dependence - independence, 9, 14, 15, 42, 44, 152
Depression, 106
Deprived, 17
Developmental cycle, ix, 99, 100
Developmental task, 9, 10, 15, 17, 18, 19, 20, 23, 26, 27, 93, 101
Diet, 20, 42
Direct-services, 22, 52
Disengagement, 16, 48
DNA, 113, 117, 118
Drugs-narcotics, 35, 77, 79

E
Ecology, 22, 49, 50

Edison, Thomas, 29
Ego, 25, 42, 43, 98
Ego - integration motivation, 70, 72, 73, 76
Emotional stability, 90, 91
Emotions, 89, 90
Environment, 21, 28, 37, 77, 78, 79, 87, 88, 98, 138
Environmental aging, 113
ESP, 69

F
Freud, S., 21, 92
Frustration, 88

G
Generation gap, 22, 54
Geriatric, xi, 7, 11, 28, 37, 40, 79, 100, 109
Ghettos for the old, 6, 22

H
Hedonistic motivation, 44, 73
Heredity, 28
Hobbies (avocations), 18, 19, 53, 95, 136, 139
Homeostatic - homeostasis, 70, 75
Hoover, J. Edgar, 121
Hormones, 114, 115, 119
Hypochondria, 146, 152
Hysteria, 105

I
Id, 25, 98
Imagery, 84
Impotence, 12
Indigence, 7, 150
Intelligence, 29
Interest in sex, 13

L
Leisure time, 18, 88
Libido, 12
Life-space, 32, 33

Life span, 13
Longevous, xii, 11, 14, 26, 38, 43, 46, 52, 53, 61, 74, 94

M

Maladjustment, 88, 89
Mania, 109
Matriarchal-patriarchal, 5, 45, 54, 94
Maturity early, 24, 88
  later, vii, 14, 19, 38, 41, 88
  middle, 38, 41
Medicare, 147, 158
Memory, 81, 82, 83, 84, 85, 86, 104
Menopause, 12, 13
Morality, 54
Mores, 22, 23, 87, 120
Motivation, 24, 29, 32, 43, 48, 49, 51, 70, 74, 75, 76, 82, 86, 100, 130

N

Narcotics-drugs, 35, 77, 79, 131
Neuroses, 88, 105, 136, 137
Neurotic, 35, 100, 102, 103, 104, 105, 106, 107, 140
New morality, 23
Non-pathological, 7, 22, 39, 40, 47, 50, 79, 101, 102, 150
Nutrition, 37

O

Obsessions, 104

P

Paranoid delusions, 104
Pathological, 15, 22, 86, 100, 104, 149
Patriarchal-matriarchal, 5, 45, 54, 94
Perception
  auditory 62
  gustatory, 64, 83
  olfactory, 63, 83
  visual, 61
  see also sensation
Personality, 25, 88, 91, 92, 93, 98, 99, 100, 101, 102, 103, 104
Pfeiffer, Eric, 13
Phobias, 105
Physiological motivation, 70, 72
Picasso, Pablo, 29
Potential, 12
Pre-retirement, 138, 151, 152

Presbycusis, 11, 60, 61, 62, 78
Presbyopia, 60, 61
Proctor, Richard C., 12
Psychoses, 88, 107, 110, 129, 136
Psychosocial motivation, 70, 71, 72
Psycho-socio-biological sex role, 9
Psychosomatic, 105
Psychotherapy, 13
Psychotic, 100, 102, 103, 104, 107, 137, 140

R

Recreation, 18
Reik, Theodor, 21
Retirement, 15, 20, 35, 47, 48, 52, 53, 74, 75, 95, 96, 97, 132, 133, 134, 137, 138, 139, 151, 152
Rule, Colter, 22

S

Schizophrenia, 108, 109
Seashore, Carl, 83
Security, 71, 95, 130, 158
Self-concept, 25, 26, 49, 52, 76, 91, 99, 138, 146, 153
Senescent-senescence, xi, 7, 11, 28, 29, 37, 40, 79, 100, 105, 106, 109, 136
Senilism, vii
Senility, xii, 152
Senium pracox, xii, 132
Sensation
  cutaneous, 65, 66, 67, 83
  kinesthetic, 11, 59, 67
  labytinthine, 68
  see also Perception
Sensory isolation, 79
Sexual activities, 105, 111, 112, 157
Sexuality, 12, 14, 44, 53
Social isolates, 103, 146
Social pressure, 30
Social rejects, 103, 146
Social Security, 139, 147, 150, 151, 158
Sociopath, 111
Sociopsychological, 47, 53
Status, 24, 30, 43, 130
Sterotype-sterotypic, ix, 5, 28, 47, 50, 53, 80, 100
Stress, 44, 88

Sub-culture of the aged, 5, 8
Superannuate, 5, 132, 135
Super-ego, 25, 98

T

Toomey, Jeanne, 21

U

Uniform crime reports, 121

V

Verdi, Guiseppe, 29
Verwoerdt, Adriaan, 13

W

Wisdom, 21, 31, 54
Withdrawal, 48, 49
Wong, Hsioh - Shan, 13